HOW TO START A
CREATIVE BUSINESS

DEDICATION

To Nancy Fulton and Medeia Cohan-Petrolino
without whom this book would not exist.
Thank you for your endless support,
encouragement (bordering on bullying), hard
work, saint like patience and endless dedication.
But most of all for your sense of humour, without
which none of the rest would be any fun.

HOW TO START A
CREATIVE BUSINESS

THE
Jargon-free
GUIDE FOR
CREATIVE ENTREPRENEURS

DOUG RICHARD

Lola Johnson

D&C
David and Charles

CONTENTS

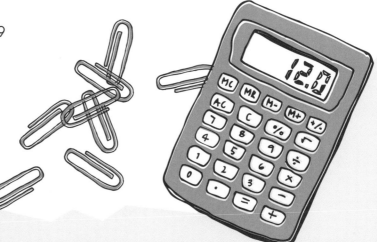

WHO IS THIS BOOK FOR?

This book is for anyone with a great idea for a creative business, whether at the ideas stage or in early development with a startup business. And startup means just that – it's just starting up.

When I talk about creative business, what I mean is a product or a service in any of the creative industries such as art, design, literature, film, music, fashion, culinary arts, performing arts, digital or craft. If there is a creative component that is the foundation stone of your business, the teaching in this book will apply to you.

At School for Creative Startups, creative people are some of our very favourite people to work with, so much so in fact that I developed our programme specifically with their needs in mind. I realised that, for creative types in particular, their business knowledge sometimes lets them down and they often think the business bit isn't their bag or that their artistry will sell itself. Sometimes they just get distracted by the more creative stuff. I've met a lot of people who have launched a business without learning the finance basics first and they have regretted it in the long run. Even some of the most successful entrepreneurs in the world have got it wrong before getting it right and in speaking with them now, they often say they wish they'd known the kinds of things we teach when they were starting out.

I'm here to give creative people the business tools, knowledge, confidence and inspiration to feel that they have it all; the gift of creativity and the business acumen to match it. I've been rolling out our method of teaching through our school since 2008 and now it's time to put it all in print.

This book will help you figure out whether your business idea can be tested, poked, stretched, intimately examined, flattened and reshaped, through a business lens. Before you take on any debt, before you go into hiding from your social life, do the work to make sure you're on the right track.

At the moment there's a lot of talk about entrepreneurship and a vision of the future where startups transform the economy and the world at large, which I believe will come true. There are stories of startups that have hit the stratosphere, ideas that have come to life and left us buzzing. There's also a scary statistic that says the majority of young businesses will fail within the first three years. The purpose of this book is to increase the likelihood of your startup's survival, sustainability and long term, its success.

I don't shy away from telling it like it is at School for Creative Startups and I want to give you as much honest advice as I can. Right off the bat, starting a business is an adventure, full of ups and downs. Sometimes it is lonely, isolating, utterly exhausting, frustrating and demoralising. Sometimes it's thrilling, joyful and financially rewarding. That's true for all entrepreneurs, even the experienced ones.

Surviving this process the first time is a bit like earning your entrepreneurial stripes. People who haven't done it underestimate just how difficult it can be and how much trial and error it can take. That's why, as a new founder, you should really only value advice from other people who have done what you're trying to do. People who have built a business from the ground up are your tribe. Only they know how incredibly painful and how utterly wonderful the journey can be.

There it is. I've said it. It's a small part of the book, but a very big point. If you're ready to ride the rollercoaster, then let's get started.

How to use this book

This book isn't a skim-through-it book, it's a take-a-breath-and-get-involved book. I've made it as easy to read and use as I can, but you'll get the most out of it if you take it on, chapter by chapter. If you read each chapter in order, and get your hands dirty with the activities, you'll get the idea first and then apply what you've learned in practical ways to the real world.

By the time you've finished the last chapter, you'll have the foundation of a very solid startup.

The format of the book is based on my ten question method. These ten questions are not equally weighted in the universe. There are some questions that are more important than others; those tend to be at the beginning. Each question gives you the answer that unlocks the following question. You'll start by answering Question One. Your answer to this question is the cornerstone for your entire enterprise. It is the monster question that brings to life all the others.

You'll find case studies at the end of each chapter to help expand on the methods I've explained and show practical applications of each lesson. I've invited some leading champions of industry and my network of contacts to tell their tales because I think people learn better from stories than from stats.

About Doug Richard

Doug Richard is a successful entrepreneur with three decades of business experience building, selling and investing in businesses of all shapes and sizes. He believes that entrepreneurs are made and not born and thrives on helping people make the leap and set up their own business.

Doug founded the original School for Startups in 2008, and through it nearly 20,000 people have learned the vital business skills they need to succeed in business. In 2010 he established School for Creative Startups, a tailor-made programme for creative people, low on jargon, packed with practical information and one-to-one support. Doug endeavours to make business education accessible, taking a wry, candid, practical, upbeat approach to a subject.

Doug is forever fine-tuning his methods and exploring new ways of engaging students to make the greatest impact. He plays an integral role in delivering curricula during boot camp and throughout the year. Additionally he regularly hosts one-to-one surgeries and advises students, chairs the School for Creative Startups Angel Society and often advises government on the best approaches to supporting British startups. You might, however, know him best from his two year stint as an angel investor on the BBC's *Dragons' Den*.

You can follow Doug on Twitter @dougrichard

School for Creative Startups

School for Creative Startups is an interactive course delivering all the business know-how that creative people need to build sustainable startups, without all the technical gibberish, pesky acronyms and theoretical rhetoric. It's just the stuff you need to know to grow your own successful startup, taught the way you like to learn it.

Whether you've got a growing kitchen-table business, hardcore hobby you'd like to make money from or just a brilliant idea bubbling away, School for Creative Startups can help you learn the basic business skills and awesome shortcuts to get you and your business up and running. You can follow School for Creative Startups on Twitter @creatives4s and visit our website at www.schoolforcreativestartups.com

INTRODUCTION
A PEP TALK FROM DOUG
(READ THIS FIRST!)

The thing that frustrates me most about creative professionals is their lack of self-belief as business owners. It's as if the act of creativity precludes them from starting a business. I don't believe this is true. Business acumen won't sully or corrupt creative talent, it merely allows creative people to do what they want to do, and make a living doing it.

I believe we're entering a golden age of creativity and that the next great revolution is a creative one. The ability to create – and to curate – is growing in value and will come to define the future economy.

Forget what you've heard. If you're a creative professional – if you have a creative product or service to offer – then this is a wonderful time to start a business.

There's a myth that people are born entrepreneurial (they aren't) and there's a naïve assumption that you have to have significant cash to start a business (you don't). I'd argue that no one is born an entrepreneur. Entrepreneurs can be made and entrepreneurship is a set of skills that can be taught. That's what this book is all about. This book will help you to start a sustainable, viable creative business.

We've taught just shy of 20,000 people through the School in the UK and beyond – we've taken the message on the road to Romania and Nigeria and we're getting invitations all the time to share our teaching in other countries. We hope to inspire and support entrepreneurship all over the world and empower creatives to make a living doing what they love.

Whatever your creative talent or passion, you can apply these business basics. It's all about getting the basics right. Once you learn how to build one startup, following the principles in this book, you know how to build a dozen.

I wish you the very best of luck.

Doug Richard

THE FUNDAMENTALS
MYTH-BUSTING AND A FEW HOME TRUTHS

Not all businesses are created equal.
Some enterprises are easier to start, easier to run, easier to scale, easier to turn profitable. That's just how it is. A good business is based on information, analysis and insight, not speculation or opinion.

Not all business owners share the same goal.
What's your dream? Is it wealth? Power? Freedom? Your first, instinctive answer to this question is usually the right one. Discover your motivation. Announce your goal. There's no shame in starting a business because you want to get rich but just be aware that only a small percentage of businesses will actually achieve that goal. If you do want to get rich, are you creating a business that can scale, that has the potential to go BIG? Can you see a path from your business idea to your goal? Is your business the right kind of business to get you to your goal? Does that path exist?

Starting and running your business is easier if you don't reinvent the world.
You're not inventing your business so much as you're discovering your business. The humility of business is that you have to go into the world and ask people if you're doing something that they care about. You don't need to reinvent the wheel. Your invention might be a new pricing model, or a new distribution channel. Most successful startups are based on a single innovation or effective use of existing production. If you're making great ice cream that's made right in front of your eyes, make it in familiar flavours. Resist the urge to innovate everything. Introducing something new and wonderful is easier and cheaper if you use, as much as possible, existing solutions for marketing, sales, production and delivery.

You don't have to be good at maths to start a business.
Starting a business really only requires the four fundamental mathematical skills: addition, subtraction, multiplication and division. Even if you struggle with maths, you can do these simple sums with a calculator. That's all you need to know. With those four basic skills you can evaluate opportunities, track successes and diagnose failures.

You don't need a business *plan* to start a business.
A business *plan* is a smart and sassy document you write for investors, lenders or potential partners that gives them some understanding of your business so they can make a decision to support it. A business *model* is the practical understanding of how it will work. This is something you do need and answering my ten key questions will help you to create your business model.

You don't need to be afraid of what data and analysis will tell you about your business.
Sometimes entrepreneurs fail to do any market research or hard thinking about their business before they start investing lots of time and that is almost always a mistake. Data and analysis is a gift of insight. It helps you shape your big ideas. You can't build a business unless you have a solid foundation and you need to do the lab work to experiment, test, develop and evolve your thinking. Running focus groups or test trading at market stalls gives you a chance to meet the public – your potential customers – and get

real feedback before investing time and money into something that isn't quite right or worse, totally wrong. Friends and family don't count! They love you, so they'll (probably) love your creation unconditionally.

You don't need heaps of cash to start a business.

It's a common complaint of the aspiring entrepreneur that they have a great idea but no one is giving them money to start the business. People rarely pay for ideas. There is a lot that you can do to start a business before you need much capital and you have a tremendous opportunity in the 21st century to start a business online at very little cost. Ask yourself if funding is really a prerequisite or if you can scale down to get things moving.

Business is not about resilience.

It's not about clinging to your idea in the face of the naysayers and the gloom-mongers because you know it to be brilliant. Tenacity is a worthy character trait but there is also great sense and humility in knowing when to let go. Listen to the advice of people who have started a successful enterprise themselves and don't be shackled to your business idea. Know when to walk away or when to keep iterating and evolving your ideas until you hit on something that really gets people jumping.

And finally...

Business is not that complicated.

All you have to do is make a sustainable profit, and profit simply means that you make more than you spend. Some people think the size of the business is important – it isn't – only the size of the profit. And whilst we're talking about profit, let's be clear that profit isn't a dirty word. It's a wonderful thing, it means your business has found a way to give people something that they want. Furthermore, a sustainable profit gives you the creative freedom you need to keep pleasing them, and yourself, for years to come.

THE TEN QUESTIONS

The Ten Questions are part of a method to help you understand what it is that you do. The act of answering them will help you to define and refine your big idea. Your success in answering them will determine how prepared you are to run your business. The Ten Questions will help you work out if you've got your business model right and if not, what it will take to get it right. The outcome of answering these ten questions is your battle plan.

You may be wondering how all creative enterprises can fit the framework of this method. Well, in reality, the commonalities of creative enterprises far outweigh their differences. Whilst each creative entrepreneur will look to their own industry and apply specific industry knowledge to their business, they will also need to get the basics right.

The Ten Questions we'll be exploring are:

ONE

The Proposition: What do you do that people need or want? How do you know that your product is answering a need or fulfilling a desire?

TWO

The Customer and The Market: Who are your customers? Where do you find your customers? What are your customers' attributes and what are your market segments? How do you prioritise your market segments?

THREE

The Competition: Who are you up against? What can you learn from your competitors? How can you compete?

FOUR

The Industry: What do you have in common with the competition? What trends are impacting your industry and how can you predict future trends?

FIVE

The Channel: What are the different routes to finding customers? How do you reach your customers? What are the different ways for you to connect your company to your customers?

SIX

The Relationship: What financial relationship do you want to have with your customers? Do you want to sell your product by subscription, via a payment plan, as a fee for service or as a product people buy for a fixed price?

SEVEN

The Pricing Model: How much should you charge for your product or service? What are your customers willing to pay? What are the other business costs to factor into your pricing model?

EIGHT

The Key Partner: Who is your key partner? How can suppliers, distributors and marketing companies become key partners? Who can you bring on board to help you deliver your product or service?

NINE

The Asset: What is your key asset? What do you have to your advantage, to help you win customers? Is it physical, intellectual, human or financial?

TEN

The Key Competency: What activities must your business be good at in order to prosper? What skills and experience do you bring to the business?

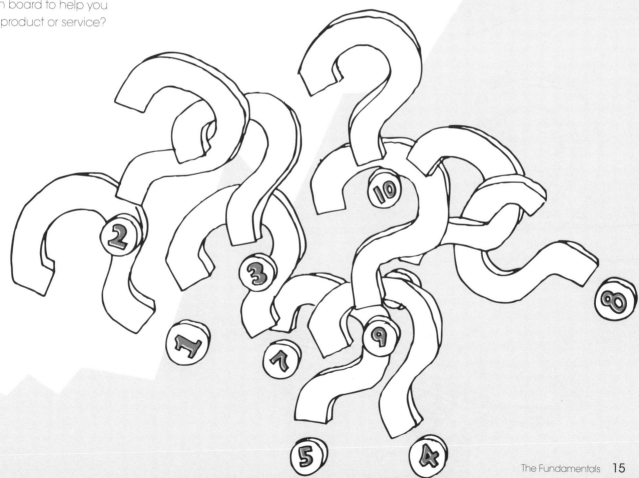

CHAPTER 1: THE PROPOSITION

WHAT DO YOU DO THAT PEOPLE NEED OR WANT?

THE PROPOSITION: WHAT DO YOU DO THAT PEOPLE NEED OR WANT?

This is a tricky question because often it isn't what you think. It's not the most obvious feature of the product or service you plan to sell. This is the question that regularly trips people up. I'll give you an example.

One of my students came to see me and when I asked him, 'What do you do, that people need or want?' he told me this: 'I make gluten-free, dairy-free muffins.'

He thought he had answered the question. He had told me what he produced and what was special about his product. But he didn't tell me *why* people would need or want his product. So why would they?

We talked more about his product. He told me that most gluten-free, dairy-free muffins – the vegan kind – don't taste as good as regular muffins. It's hard to make a delicious, moist, muffin without using dairy products. But my student had found a solution and the muffins he made were delicious.

So what he actually produced – the thing that people wanted – was *delicious*, vegan and gluten-free muffins. The fact that they were delicious was the point. That was the marketing hook. They were delicious *and* they were gluten-free and vegan. That's what he was selling, that was the promise and that's what he should have told me was the one thing that people wanted that he could provide.

All brands have a promise. Your brand is a delicate relationship with the customer that's based on trust that you will deliver on your promise. So what's your promise? When you're thinking about your product or the service you offer, think beyond its obvious, operational use. What is it that your customers need or want? Tease out the meaning and the real value to your customer. Find the emotional connection. Identify the catalyst that will convert a fan of your work into a real, paying customer. What do you do that people need or want? That is the fundamental cornerstone of your business. Don't ever lose sight of it.

STARTUP STORY: ETHOS

QUENTIN CLARK

HEAD OF SUSTAINABILITY AND ETHICAL SOURCING AT WAITROSE

www.waitrose.com

Wallace Waite, Arthur Rose and David Taylor opened their first small grocery shop at 263 Acton Hill, West London, in 1904. That little grocery shop became Waitrose, one of the country's leading food retailers. The John Lewis Partnership acquired the business in 1937, opening the first Waitrose supermarket in 1955. Today there are 280 branches of Waitrose, and the company employs over 37,000 people. Waitrose holds a Royal Warrant from Her Majesty The Queen.

Waitrose is a co-owned business, leading to a higher level of employee engagement than other companies because our staff are also effectively our shareholders. That is why they are called 'Partners'. All companies have a culture of some description but they often struggle to articulate it. This was our task and to address it we created a way to pull it all together that was comprehensible and clear to all our stakeholders; staff, customers and suppliers. John Spedan Lewis, our founder, defined our business principles of fairness, honesty and hard work right at the start of The Partnership in his book 'Fairer Shares'. So, in some sense, we've been using 'the Waitrose Way' since the very beginning, it's always been fundamentally a core part of how we did business.

The Waitrose Way is inward facing in that it influences the way that people think about what they do in their day-to-day work; it's outward facing in that we can take it to our customers to talk about what is important to us and to them. It's also backward facing to our suppliers as it's vital that we engage our suppliers in delivering our values too. We know that what the customer sees is not Waitrose but what Waitrose sells and how it sells it, so our values have to be communicated throughout the chain, from our suppliers, through our Waitrose stores and out to our customers.

There are four pillars to the Waitrose Way. The first, 'Championing British', is all about celebrating British sourcing, supporting sustainable British agriculture and the British economy. We try to contribute constructively to the political debate and we're involved in Government consultations.

The second pillar is 'Treading Lightly', which is about how we are reducing our environmental footprint, cutting our carbon waste reduction and new technology, like using electrical vehicles. The latest generation of Waitrose stores are powered with renewable energy derived from wood chips. This pillar is also about sustainability and the sustainable sourcing of products such as fish, soya and palm oil.

The third pillar is 'Treating People Fairly', which is within the supply chain – in using fairly traded products sourced through the Waitrose Foundation, or other schemes such as FairTrade and in our communities through Community Matters, which is our community outreach programme. You might have seen the green chips in Waitrose stores that we give to customers who can then vote on the community issue that matters to them. We convert the votes to cash. Customers love the idea that they can vote to support local causes.

We're galvanising community support, encouraging our customers who share our values to join with us, and donations through food banks are business as usual for us as an example.

The last pillar is 'Living Well', which is about dietary advice, healthy eating and well-being. This is the pillar that covers all the work we are doing in reducing salt, saturated fat and so on, but we are very mindful that we are talking about food that people enjoy eating so we have been careful to do that without compromising the taste.

Once we had created the four pillars, we looked at how best to communicate them, both internally and externally. It's also a recurring theme in all our publications that are available in-store, like *Waitrose Weekend* or *Waitrose Kitchen* and in our house journalism through *The Chronicle* and *The Gazette*.

We've created a sort of cultural spine around the Waitrose Way that our teams can use as a reference for their own behaviour. It helps to have a guide to how we do business and how we treat people and even though we're now a large company, everyone shares that state of mind. Any teams that are business planning will be guided by the Waitrose Way. We've also created a series of awards, reflecting the pillars and aims of the Waitrose Way that we give to suppliers who have excelled in delivering these values.

Customers will shop with you if you are a known brand, if you're nearby or if you're selling what they want. We've analysed what customers want and it really comes down to understanding value. We've tackled the price comparison with other supermarkets through things like 'Tesco Brand Price Match' where we make sure that branded goods that are sold in Waitrose and Tesco will be the same price. But it's also true that where products take into account animal welfare, quality and ethical sourcing, there are price implications. The same thing that produces sustainability often also produces the great taste and quality. Customers will buy food that tastes the best and the sourcing of those products in an ethical way can have a huge impact on this higher quality and so there is a real win-win. But it is much more than that. It's all about the triple bottom line. Reducing carbon emissions and preserving resources saves the company money. A company that is not doing these things is not competitive for long, so really, there is no other way to do business. It's not just Corporate Social Responsibility, it's about selling the very best and good business sense all rolled into one.

Our business model is rooted in long-term relationships with our suppliers because we need high-quality products, produced to our specific standards, which are continually available to our customers, and we need our suppliers to have the confidence in the future to invest in the quality and values of our products. In a real sense we are what we sell, so those relationships are built and continue over the longer term.

Social media is an important new means of communication and we have a team of people who manage the Waitrose Facebook and Twitter accounts through which we invite customer conversation and suggestions. Financial pundits have been known to say that in a recession, people will walk away from our type of business in search of the cheapest price but that's not so. We've found customers actually walk towards us in a recession. They value what's important, they value the experience, they aren't eating out as much but still want to eat well and be treated well. If anything, in thinking more about how they spend their money they look closely at the food they are buying and make decisions in favour of true value, which is so much more than the price; it takes into account quality and how that food has been produced. I think it may also be about how the businesses they choose to use are supporting the bigger issues of society. The IGD (Institute of Grocery Distribution) invites all supermarkets to contribute their sales figures and in return shows how each are doing in the market. We've consistently outperformed our competitors, which shows that people value our proposition: quality food produced in the right way.

Our job is never done because there is always more to do – there are always innovations in food technology and sourcing and ethical issues that keep the business moving forward. The minute you think you've 'got it', you've lost it!

Your business promise, in a nutshell

A lot of what I'm talking about in this first chapter is being able to distil your big idea into a bite-sized nugget so that everyone that you tell about your business can 'get it' immediately. Sometimes the more you talk around the idea, the more you elaborate, the more you'll confuse people or they'll lose interest. You need to communicate the value of your business in a single, simple promise that explains *who, delivers what, to whom, where*. Entrepreneurs who can't describe their business in a single statement or tell people a story that explains its purpose will have a hard time finding customers, industry partners, or employees. Remember that your promise and your story define your brand.

GET YOUR HANDS DIRTY
Try this: Write down your promise to customers in a single, simple sentence about the length of a tweet.

- It should imply how you have solved a problem or fulfilled a desire.
- It should identify **who** delivers the value. Are you working alone or as part of a team?

- It should define **what** the company does in the simplest terms. Are you selling products created by others, manufacturing products that others will sell, or delivering a bespoke service?
- It should define exactly **who** your customers are. Are you selling to families, businesses, or wealthy young professionals?
- If possible, it should define exactly **where** you will find your customers. Are you selling to people online, in shops, or to networks of friends?

Every successful creative startup delivers something people need or want. How do you know people want what you sell? Easy – ask them.

Asking your potential customers what they want is one of the simplest and most important pieces of research for any startup.

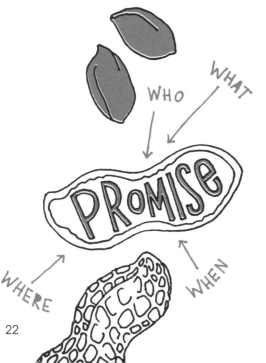

WHO WHAT

PROMISE

WHERE WHEN

EXAMPLES
'We sell designer straw hats to families at the beach.'
'We help young brides have the wedding dress of their dreams by creating bespoke, affordable, antique lace dresses.'
'We deliver live events for teenage audiences with educational, interactive musical experiences.'

GET YOUR HANDS DIRTY

Try this: Speak to potential customers and get their feedback.

1. Try contacting members of your network to come and view your product or sign up for a small booth at a trade show or fair where your competitors regularly sell their wares.

2. Present your prototype or sample service or, if you don't have a prototype, create marketing materials that describe what you plan to deliver. Let potential customers see your product or marketing materials, in exchange for feedback.

3. To get the most from your audience it's worth running some kind of competition. Ask visitors to answer three questions about your product or service and add their email address to a slip of paper that they pop into a closed box from which you draw a winning name. Make sure you ask open questions where you can learn from the answers, such as which is your favourite product and why? How much would you pay for it? Where would you expect to buy this?

4. Focus groups are easy to run and can be really fun and useful. The promise of wine or food could entice a great group of people to trial your new service and then feed back their thoughts. Make sure you reach the right audience with your focus group or market stall. Take the time to find the right customer group, and the right marketplace. You want to canvass opinion from the people who might buy your product or service.

5. Social media is another way to gauge the response from potential customers. Showcase new products to your loyal followers and listen to their feedback.

6. Collect all the feedback and refine your pitch until those potential customers begin asking you to contact them when you do have something to sell. Ask each person you talk to for referrals to others who may be interested in your business. Collect contact information for the customers who seem interested in what you are offering. You might even get pre-orders for what you plan to sell.

Ask yourself:

- Do people accurately understand your product or service after reviewing your marketing materials?
- When they describe your product to you, do they describe it correctly? If so, what words do they use? Write these words down and use them in your pitch to new customers.

ANALYSE CUSTOMER RESPONSES AND LOOK FOR PATTERNS

- Where do your customers expect to buy your product or service?
- When do your customers expect to buy your product or service?
- What events motivate them to buy your project or service?
- Why do they prefer your product or service to your competitors' offer?
- What language do they use to describe the value you deliver?
- What need or desire does your product or service fulfil for those who decide to buy what you sell?
- What advantages, or benefits, does your product or service deliver to your customers?
- What makes them decide to buy?
- What does your product or service allow them to do?
- How is it different to your competition?
- What would make it even better?
- Where would they look if they wanted to buy your product or service?
- Where would they expect to see what you sell being promoted?
- What search terms would they use to find it on an Internet search engine such as Google?
- How much would they expect to pay for your product or service?
- What do they pay for your competitors' products or services?
- Is the current price accurate?
- Which specific companies do they think of when they see your product or hear about your service?

- What relevant characteristics do those who most like the product or service share?
- Where can you reach pools of these people for free or little cost in the months/years to come?
- Where do they live?
- Where do they work?
- What do they do?
- Where do they shop?
- What related products or services do they buy?

You can alter your pitch and product based on all the feedback from potential customers. This helps you to work out what will sell best and how to pitch it, well before you've invested too much time and money. Have you created something people want or need?

Here's the challenge: If you can't get positive feedback, pre-orders, or requests for more information from a hundred or more potential customers in under a month, you'll probably find it pretty difficult to sell products or services to them in the months or years to come. When this happens, it is either because your product or service isn't something people value or because you can't effectively pitch it to them. Either of these things will kill your enterprise so you have to solve this problem before you move on to the rest of the steps in this book.

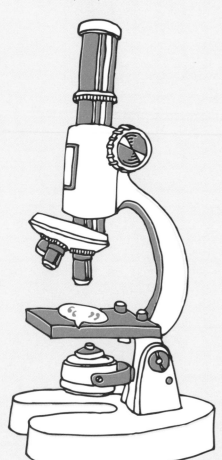

TELLING YOUR STORY

Storytelling isn't optional when starting a business – it's critical.

The stories you tell help people to look beyond the risk and the lack of proof that your business will succeed. You might only have a business idea and a bunch of contacts at the moment so your story is most likely a fictitious one. But you can still paint a picture of the future to help people see the world – and the opportunity – the way you see it. Tell your story to people so that they become your fans. These people are your cheerleaders, your Formula 1 pit team, your business advocates and evangelists. They're your unofficial agents, PR managers and sales reps. Tell your investors, creditors, employees and customers the story and make them want to become characters in the narrative you're creating.

Shape your story, practise your patter, sound the fanfare: here is your business and with it come the answers, the solution, the enjoyment and delight. You are the hero of your story. You are the hero that solves the problem or fulfils the desire!

GET YOUR HANDS DIRTY
Try this: Write the story behind your business.

THERE ARE DIFFERENT WAYS THAT YOU CAN APPROACH YOUR STORY:

Writing the story behind a business is often a defining moment for an entrepreneur because it captures the intent behind the business. The mechanics of launching a startup often distract us from the importance of what we are trying to achieve. A story, particularly one told repeatedly, reminds us of our objectives and strengthens our commitment to our purpose, our promise and our brand.

ONE

Why did you start your business? Most people see starting a business as brave. Describing how you decided to take such a step is a great way to introduce your enterprise.

EXAMPLE

I'd been working for website developers since 2002 and found that many clients had no idea how to engage their customers in creating their own products. I began creating those websites and recently started a new business where I help my clients to engage their customers through fresh, interactive design.

TWO

Who will your business help? This story is often used by social enterprises and charities and is often about emotional connection to the customer.

EXAMPLE

More than one fifth of all children in the UK live below the poverty line. Many go to bed hungry every night and yet most come from families where both parents work. Our social enterprise runs a series of concerts and events that informs people about domestic poverty and uses donated funds to aid impoverished children.

THREE

How will your product be used? This is often used by entrepreneurs who deliver products and services to other artists and businesses.

EXAMPLE

A 13th-century blue, a 17th-century yellow, a 19th-century green… Fisher Authentic Pigments are created by master chemists to exactly match the chemical properties of paints used throughout the ages. Founded by restoration experts who have worked with leading museums worldwide, Barbara and Antoine Fisher have made it their mission to preserve the work of old masters.

A final word on the proposition

I created a business called Library House, which was a business information and consulting company. We created an über-database of every company in the tech industry across Europe which meant that we had a unique insight into what was going on in the industry and we could share that valuable insight with our customers who were looking to place the next big bets in tech investment. We gave our customers access to the über-database and then we started running events to bring together companies looking for investment from potential investors. They were slick events, we got fantastic feedback and our customers loved coming to them. We charged companies a single, flat fee to get access to the database and to come to our events. So far, so good, right?

Then we decided to change our model by charging customers one fee for access to the database, where we were focusing most of our efforts, and one (significantly lower) fee for access to our events. What happened? The majority of our customers shifted to the lower pricing model, opting to pay the lower fee for the events and forgo access to the database. Our income dropped overnight. Turns out the only thing our customers wanted was to come to the events. I hadn't asked my customers that one simple question: I hadn't asked them what it was that I did, that they needed or wanted. If I had asked the question, chances are my customers would have told me how much they valued the real world, face-to-face meetings with investors and exciting investment opportunities. I could have developed a brilliant events strategy based on that insight alone but I didn't have that knowledge because I hadn't asked. I got so enthused by the database and we worked so hard to get it right that I thought the database had value in the market that it just didn't have. I saw value where there wasn't any; I thought I knew what my customer wanted without asking.

My point is that any one of us can get the proposition wrong. I got it wrong. And Library House wasn't even my first business.

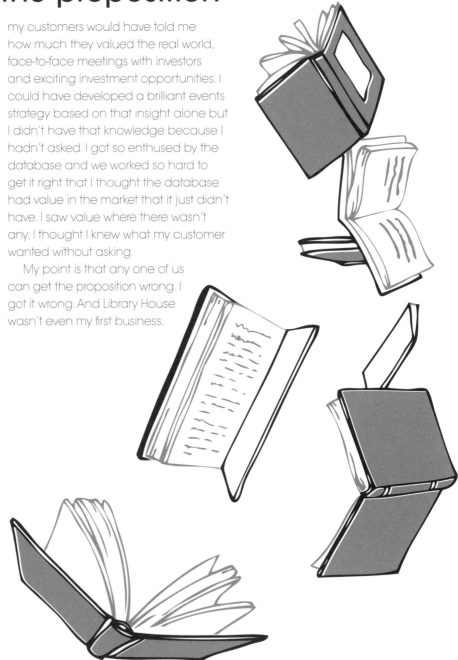

STARTUP STORY: THE PROPOSITION

ROSIE WOLFENDEN
CO-FOUNDER, TATTY DEVINE
www.tattydevine.com

Rosie Wolfenden and Harriet Vine set up Tatty Devine in 1999, and the brand has become a cult classic of British fashion with its witty, offbeat jewellery designs. Every piece is designed by the duo and 99% of the jewellery is made by hand in Tatty Devine's own workshops. Each year, two main collections are launched at London Fashion Week. Tatty Devine has two London boutiques and over 100 stockists worldwide. Rankin shot a dress covered in Tatty Devine brooches to celebrate 25 years of London Fashion Week, and *Dazed & Confused* magazine has listed Tatty Devine as one of the 50 coolest brands in the world as chosen by the Cool Brands' Council.

We started Tatty Devine just at a grassroots level; it was very organic. Harriet and I met at art school and we really hit it off. Neither of us wanted a 'proper' job but we didn't have a business background and we didn't have any investment. We made fun and colourful stuff to wear for parties and that's how it all began. Then we stumbled across some leather samples and started making leather bracelets that we sold from a stall in Portobello Road. They were really popular, so we made some more. We surfed the crest of a wave really, making things that we loved and they seemed to sell. We made fun, colourful, statement jewellery; the stuff that we wanted to wear and that didn't cost the Earth to buy. Our style has always been very fresh and authentic.

We always had the desire to make original products and it seemed to strike a chord at that time. We started in the late nineties when to us fashion felt quite stripped back, dull and bland, with a lot of beige and grey. In contrast, our designs were very bold and our aesthetic deliberately different. There really wasn't anything out there that was similar to what we were doing. I worked part-time at Steinberg and Tolkien, a vintage store on London's King's Road, and I was inspired by the glamour of vintage; it felt exciting and different as vintage hadn't quite crept into the mainstream consciousness yet. Referencing vintage shapes and styles – which we did a lot in our designs – just wasn't commonplace. Harriet and I used to get our clothes from charity shops because we didn't have much money and were always striving for interesting looks. Now there are loads of vintage, retro and second-hand shops to choose from, which didn't exist before.

Some successes seemed to happen almost by chance. A stylist came into

Steinberg and Tolkien when I was working there and loved the headband I was wearing. She asked where she could get one for a magazine shoot and it was actually one of ours, a Tatty Devine creation. So I told her about it and I really sold her on Tatty Devine and she wanted to use it in the shoot – that magazine that the stylist was working on turned out to be *Vogue*! It was an opportunity really – a lot of great things have happened from chance meetings like that, and from us seizing those opportunities. We have a real drive to talk about what we do and to get people as excited about it as we are. After that we had a number of approaches: Urban Outfitters, then Whistles, then Harvey Nichols – that was in September 1999 and they approached us by saying, 'We need some young, fun accessories that aren't available on the high street at the moment...'

What we make is all about individualism and appeals to people who want to be a bit different. We have such a diverse audience, from the fashionable 25-year-old to the stylish 80-year-old. There's one group of customers that has grown up with us and then another group that has found us by chance. We've done focus groups to find out more about our customer and found that generally our customers are female, independent, cultured and educated. We also found that potential customers who didn't know us already were struck by the quality of our jewellery because it's all handmade. We built a production and fulfilment studio in Kent and it just keeps growing because of the high demand.

Being a UK company is important to us and to our identity. There's a Britishness to Tatty Devine that appeals to our customers. Harriet and I both grew up with a fondness for craft-making and a love for handmade items; that element of Britishness and our quirkiness has helped us find a niche, and find customers abroad. There is an ingrained set of references to British culture and British history in our designs and because London is such a multicultural and diverse place, we draw on that in our jewellery design. Harriet and I always ask each other about things that we have seen recently that we love and are excited by, and that informs the next collection.

We're always bombarded with offers to partner with other brands, so we're quite careful about what we want to focus on and we've said that next year we'll try to go after the partners that we want to collaborate with and look more at retail and new markets. I'd love us to explore New York, Paris, Tokyo and Melbourne, as those audiences are like our UK audiences and I think we'll do well. We might do something with Rough Trade and possibly with Bestival. The great thing about partnerships is that you can potentially reach out to a whole new audience and take advantage of somebody else's PR machine. It's a lot of fun to collaborate with other creative people and come up with something completely new and unique.

We've got a pop-up shop in Selfridges in London at the moment selling our custom-made Name Necklaces that have gone off the scale in terms of their popularity and have been worn by some famous faces. The pop-up is doing incredibly well; people love that they can get a handmade item in under half an hour and that they can watch it being crafted for them. The pop-up is going to become permanent and I'd love to roll that out across the world!

Retail has changed so much. It's not enough to just sell stuff anymore. You need to create a branded space and let people enter into your world and get engulfed by it. Retail has gone to another level, it's far more experiential and that's what the customers want; the whole immersive experience. We've started doing Tatty Devine workshops following on from the success of our jewellery-making book and it seems that people like coming to our shops and making something unique themselves, to take away – it's the full Tatty Devine experience!

NOW YOU KNOW...

- How to create a promise.
- You understand how critical it is to be able to introduce your business in one clear, simple sentence. You can now appreciate why that is your most important sales tool and your most important business management tool.
- You understand why the story behind your business is important.

Your story explains to customers, suppliers and strategic partners why you're exactly the right person to build your business.

- You've seen why customer feedback is so important. Customers respond to some promises far better than others. So start your market research early and continue it throughout the process of creating and running your business.

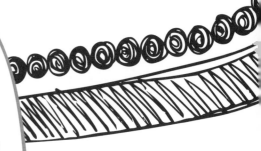

WHAT YOU'VE ACCOMPLISHED...

If you've followed the steps in this chapter you have:

- Created your promise which you can incorporate into every pitch, every interview, and every brochure. You'll have it all over your website and incorporate it into your conversations with suppliers, resellers, those you hire and strategic marketing partners.
- Developed your story you'll use in all your presentations, all your interviews, and any pitches you'll make to potential investors in years to come.
- Started the marketing research

required to ensure your company delivers a product or service people really want to buy.

- You've found members of your target market to test your business ideas on, and you've learned that most people are happy to give you their well-informed opinion if you ask simple questions and accept their answers.
- You may even have found some customers who are eager to buy what you plan to sell.

CHAPTER 2: THE CUSTOMER AND THE MARKET

WHO ARE THEY?

WHO ARE THEY?

A little piece of advice: In this book I use the term 'customers' a lot. This is a word some creative professionals find uncomfortable but if people pay for your work, they are your customers. They might also be your audience, your fans, your patrons or sponsors. Don't let the word customers put you off. We have to call them something.

JARGON BUSTER!

Markets and *market segments* can be visualised if you think of an orange. The whole orange is your *market*. The orange sections are groups of customers with something in common. These are *market segments*.

Who is the customer?

This question gives you an insight into organisations and the way they work.

If you have a product/service that solves a problem or fulfils a desire, it solves a problem or fulfils a desire *for someone*. That someone could be your customer.

Always remember that your customer is the person who pays for your product or service. They're not always the one who uses or consumes it. Sometimes people buy things for themselves; sometimes they buy things for others.

For example, mothers are the customers for people who make baby clothes. Babies wear what their mothers put on them. If you want to sell baby clothes, you have to make mums happy as well as babies because babies don't have their own credit cards.

Magazines are another example where there's a difference between the customer and the consumer. The majority of magazine publishers get most of their money from advertisers. Advertisers want to buy cheap and easy access to people who buy the kind of products and services they sell. Magazines create articles, images and other content to gather up those customers month after month. What magazines really do is sell groups of people to advertisers.

It is not uncommon for a struggling business owner to discover that the reason their business is failing is that they've been ignoring their customer since the day their business began.

MARKETS AND MARKET SEGMENTS

Sometimes creative entrepreneurs find talk of markets and market segments intimidating. It's actually not that difficult and here's why...

Imagine all of your potential customers in one place, standing in front of you. Do they all look identical? Probably not. I'm sure you could find a way to group them by age, or by gender or by their lifestyle choices, style or hobbies.

The sum of all your potential customers is called your market. Groups of customers within your market are called market segments.

Total Available Market vs Total Accessible Market

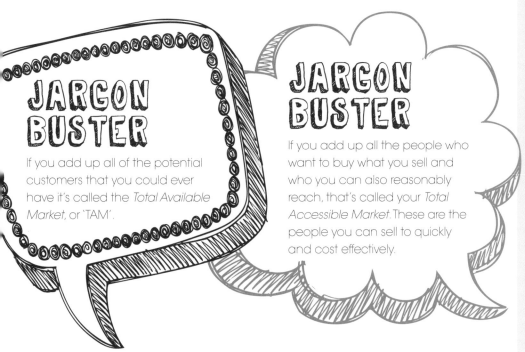

JARGON BUSTER

If you add up all of the potential customers that you could ever have it's called the *Total Available Market*, or 'TAM'.

JARGON BUSTER

If you add up all the people who want to buy what you sell and who you can also reasonably reach, that's called your *Total Accessible Market*. These are the people you can sell to quickly and cost effectively.

Not everyone is in the TAM for your company. For example, if you're selling baby clothes, your total available market is only people who have a baby or know people with babies. There are certain people who simply will never, ever buy baby clothes. They are not your customers and never will be. Your product is irrelevant to them and they are all but irrelevant to you.

Having a large Total Accessible Market is very important to a startup. It's not wise to start a business selling life-sized sculptures if you don't know anyone who buys them and can't discover any easy ways to reach that group of people. While the Total Available Market for life-sized statues might be huge, the Total *Accessible* Market is fairly small.

THE TOTAL ACCESSIBLE MARKET IS A SUBSET OF THE TOTAL AVAILABLE MARKET

As an entrepreneur you'll always want to be trying to *grow* your total accessible market and, of course, it's a number that will increase over time as your business grows.

You want to be able to sell to as many people in your *Total Available Market* (TAM) as you possibly can, so it should be one of the core goals of all your marketing, distribution and channels (I'll come onto this stuff later) to increase the number of potential customers you reach everyday.

When it comes to online marketing, your objective becomes increasing your visibility, which means making it easy for search engines and social networks to find you. The more visible you are, the larger your total accessible market becomes.

Attributes

Entrepreneurs spend a lot of time talking about their customer but they often focus on the wrong characteristics.

As a consumer, there are bits about you as a person that are relevant to the products you buy and bits about you as a person that aren't relevant at all. If we're talking about cosmetics, the fact that the customer is a woman is a relevant factor. It's a relevant characteristic or *attribute*.

A marketer of cosmetics must take into account that the majority of the market is female. But if we're talking about bicycle tools, gender isn't relevant. The really relevant *attribute* is if you ride a bike or not. Therefore the attributes you choose to describe your customer must be attributes that are relevant to that product or service.

The most common attributes that are useful ways to define customers and customer types are wealth, age and gender.

If you browse the supermarket shelves, you'll see products aimed specifically at teenage girls, young boys, middle-aged men and so on. Gender and age tend to be things we naturally use to segment people but it's not always the case. Sometimes we describe people solely by a pursuit: 'She's a cyclist' or 'She's a surfer'. Sometimes by where they live: 'He's a Londoner' or 'He lives in Manchester'. These are all potentially relevant attributes that help you to separate your customers into groups or segments to market to them effectively. That's called market segmentation.

There are more formal ways of separating customers or audiences into groups by social grade or implied wealth (meaning their income and/or earnings). You might hear terms like 'ABC1' as a definition of a customer type. The ABC system is a classification system based on occupation, created by the National Readership Survey (NRS, www.nrs.co.uk). The system has been widely interpreted to create customer profiles or definitions for consumer targeting and market research.

The letters A, B, C and so on are used as a shorthand to describe different customer types, based on their social grade in society and the apparent wealth of that social grade..

Social grade	Occupation
A	higher managerial, administrative or professional
B	intermediate managerial, administrative or professional
C1	supervisory or clerical, junior managerial, administrative or professional
C2	skilled manual workers
D	semi and unskilled manual workers
E	state pensioners or widows (no other earner), casual or lowest grade workers

You might hear marketing speak referring to, for example, the ABs, meaning the wealthy (As) and the near wealthy (Bs). You don't need to get hung up on the definitions, just get the gist of how the definitions apply and why they are useful.

1. Think about those customers who most often buy your product or service. What do they have in common? Take a moment to paint a picture of this 'good customer' and the attributes that will help you find and sell to them. For example: 'My customer's name is Joe, he's 37, he's into watching sports, he sits at home on the weekend drinking beer, he hasn't got a girlfriend because he's a bit of a player, he only shaves once a week, he buys a lot of lager at the off-licence down the road and sometimes goes to games…'

2. Which bits of your customer Joe's description are relevant to the product or service you are trying to sell to Joe? What aspects do you need to take into account when you're trying to market to him? What are the relevant attributes? You could say that he likes your soft cotton jumpers because they are comfortable and have team logos on them.

3. How many of these customers like Joe are there out there? That will tell you the size of Joe's market segment. How many can you reasonably reach in the course of a year?

4. Repeat this process four or five times to identify each of your different market segments, and the characteristics that will allow you to quickly find and reach them. Estimate how many of these people there are. How many can you reasonably expect to reach in a year?

What you've just done is identify your total available market which is all the people you can sell to, your market segments which are all the 'good customers' you've identified, and the number you can easily reach within the year which is your total accessible market. Take a minute to consider how you intend to reach them or whether you are capable of reaching them right away – you've just described your access to the market plan.

Ta-dah! Something that seems incredibly complex and mysterious becomes something really quite straightforward.

STARTUP STORY: THE MARKET

WILL RAMSAY

WILL'S ART WAREHOUSE AND AFFORDABLE ART FAIR

www.wills-art.com/home

www.affordableartfair.com

Founder and CEO of the Affordable Art Fairs worldwide, Will began his entrepreneurial adventure in 1996 with Will's Art Warehouse based in Putney, London, which showcases a diverse selection of affordable art in a friendly environment. He went on to create the Affordable Art Fair which takes place in Amsterdam, Bristol, Brussels, New York, Milan, Singapore, Hamburg, Mexico City, Rome, Seattle, Stockholm and Hong Kong. Globally, over a million people have visited an Affordable Art Fair, buying over £155 million of art.

When I was in my mid-twenties I used to go around commercial galleries and felt that I wasn't being helped to learn about art. Sometimes the staff ignored me, sometimes there was no information about the artist or that information was difficult to find; it was silent and off-putting as a cultural experience. I felt the art world was really difficult for people who weren't confident about their art tastes. There was the potential to follow the model the wine world had created – to expand the market beyond people who knew about wine (or in this case, art) by removing the jargon, making the product accessible,

having an honest conversation about it. The art world was the most backward within the retail sector in terms of attracting new customers.

My first endeavour was Will's Art Warehouse, a slight borrowing of Majestic Wine Warehouse. I was fortunate to inherit some shares and I was able to get a £100,000 overdraft facility by putting the shares up as security; I was prepared to risk this inheritance to set up the business I believed in. Incidentally, I was £96,000 into the overdraft about 18 months after opening! Luckily at that point it started coming together. In retrospect, I should have tested the market in a smaller way first. I should have organised one exhibition, rented a gallery space or exhibited at an art fair but I brazenly went ahead full throttle. I'd recommend to startups that they test the market in a small way by exhibiting at a trade fair. It might cost you £5,000 for a stand but it's well worth doing because you're testing your product and understanding your customer. Speak to other people in the industry about their customers and how they attract and retain them.

My first few exhibitions were far too varied and there was no cohesion to it. I didn't have the right product range – I didn't know enough about my product. I did a bit of research, spoke to friends about my idea, but over-confidently pressed ahead with my hunch. Statistics was an element of my course at university and I learned about quantitative and qualitative research. Although I didn't use it enough in the beginning, I think every entrepreneur

should understand those research methods. I approached one guy who had a gallery who was a friend of a friend. I showed him the business plan – I think I was there about ten minutes – and he said it would never work. I was very gratified when, about four years later, he rang and asked for a stand at the Affordable Art Fair!

Agile Development is a really important concept and that's something I did unwittingly. If I hadn't done that I would have run out of money. One of my artists whose work I was exhibiting in one of the first shows came to see my exhibition space and said, 'What a great place for a party!' and I thought, what a great idea to get the business known and to show art in a different way. We became more than a gallery, we were a venue for private parties with art on the walls. That model became a third of the business turnover and kept me going. It got my name out there, and put my gallery on the map as a destination. I'd say to any young business, don't be hell-bent on doing your Plan A and sticking rigidly to it. Adapt the product, be prepared to change your opinion of who is your customer. Very rarely is there a product that doesn't need evolving; it should be constantly updated to stay ahead of competitors, trends and technological changes.

The Affordable Art Fair came two years after Will's Art Warehouse. That

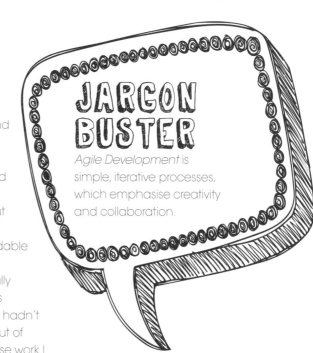

was a much greater turnover business so a greater risk but by that time Will's Art Warehouse had been my market test. It wouldn't have seemed professional for me to send a survey around to all the galleries in Britain asking, 'What do you think of this idea?' – I had to show a certain amount of knowledge and confidence. I'd had two years of understanding the customer and the product and I also talked to other galleries and asked them what they thought. I exhibited at the Glasgow Art Fair which was useful for me to be known as a fellow gallerist, rather than an exhibition organiser who didn't understand the market.

Affordable Art Fair has more than one customer. We have the galleries who exhibit with us and the visitors who buy from those galleries. We also have our sponsors, they're another customer. I started off in the world of

Business to Consumer (B2C) with Will's Art Warehouse and I'm now more B2B (Business to Business) with the Affordable Art Fair. We get more revenue from the galleries paying per square footage to exhibit at the fair than from the visitors paying entrance fees. I think B2B is so much easier; it's less competitive.

Our B2C customer in the public sphere is quite broad-range. It's rarely someone aged under 25; the larger market for us is aged 30–60. It helps if they are an owner-occupier because they have more pride in their home and want it to look good. It also helps if they have a reasonable amount of money to spend. The average price of art at the fair is £700 but the range is from £40 to £4,000. Some visitors will spend £20,000 on five pieces; some might spend £200. They might also buy it in instalments at £30 a month. We've tried to highlight to visitors that galleries do offer paying by instalments, and that they could commission something similar. We do a big push on educating people about art, including doing on-site demonstrations at the fair. I'd recommend that if you're exhibiting at an art or trade fair, you do a demonstration. Don't just have the finished product there. If you can't demo it, have storyboards to show the process and get customer feedback.

With our B2B customer (the galleries) we always try to approach the right person at the right time. We think about when in the week they might be snowed under and won't want to be considering a new event and what

time of year is best too. We advertise in the trade press and I think it's vital to have a decent website with information about who you are and what you know. If it's a brand-new event, we'll make sure that the galleries realise that it isn't just about making sales; it's about the contacts they make. We help them learn more about their products and their customers. We give our galleries invites for them to distribute to their networks and a ready-made email to send to their customers. We make it as easy as possible for them to spread the word. If customers are taking a risk on something new, it's important we thank them for taking that leap of faith with us. We have a competition between our different fairs to see who can get the most Facebook likes! We try and make it fun. We have our business values, which are listening, efficient, energy, caring, evolving and fun. We also follow the seven Ps: Prior Preparation and Planning Prevents Piss-Poor Performance! Ultimately we understand our brand in order that our customers can make sense of it.

With B2C the whole marketing mix is important. We always engage a PR company. We've thought about doing PR in-house but we've always come back to the fact that PR companies have better contacts with the press, they know more about what will attract journalists and they're more time efficient because they'll approach journalists with a suite of ideas, of which ours is one. We get a lot of business customers who have seen

our consumer marketing – don't ever forget that your business customers don't exist in a bubble, they are also Joe Public outside of business hours. We're always aware that our invite to a gallery opening might come with 20 other invites so if our customers see the invite and also see a Tube poster or a magazine article about the same event, it raises our invite above the other 20. We also use networks hugely. We call up businesses and ask if they want to give their staff an evening out and we incentivise them with half-price tickets or some offer. I think you can waste a lot of money on advertising to your customer if you're not strategic about it. We think about the size of the ad and whether we really need it or whether a simple listing is enough. Make your buck work harder, I always say.

We've found it's important to continually test customer satisfaction and we use SurveyMonkey (www.surveymonkey.com) a lot. We give exhibitor questionnaires out; we also call exhibitors to see how they found the fair. We do visitor questionnaires as well. We think carefully about how long it will take the customer to fill out our surveys and how we can incentivise them; can we give them a free ticket to next year's show for example, or a bottle of champagne. I heard someone once say, 'A customer is twice as likely to leave you if they have been treated with indifference.' The customer is always right – or rather, they need to think they're always right! It may be galling to give your customer a full refund on their product when in your opinion they've made the wrong buying decision but if you look after them, they'll come back. It costs a lot more to find a new customer than it does to keep an existing one happy. I've found it's worthwhile to go the extra mile and treat all our customers as individuals. Try and find out a little bit more about each customer. Do they play golf and have a handicap of 6? Do they have two children who are six and four? Those are the conversation starters, they are the personal touch. You can never underestimate what a difference that makes.

LEARNING TO SAY NO

Startups are different from established businesses. Established businesses have enough time, money and employees to juggle multiple market segments. As a startup, you'll need to choose just one of your market segments to sell to first. You'll pick one battleground, one tiny market to take, and succeed there first. Why?

Because the biggest issue facing a startup is that it's under-resourced. You need to get going, you need to get the business turning and you can't afford to spread yourself too thinly. This is a lesson in focus and concentration and it starts with narrowing down your choice of market segment.

Entrepreneurs, particularly the creative ones, often squirm away from targeting a single market segment. They're enthusiastic, eager and ambitious – three great qualities. Sound familiar? Trouble is, you'll fail if you simultaneously try to take advantage of all of your opportunities at once. You're too small right now.

The act of being a successful entrepreneur is the act of having willpower and discipline. You need to learn to say no. This – the question of your customer and the market – is one of the big issues to test your willpower and resolve. You want to sell to everyone and you want to do it right away, but you simply can't.

Time and again entrepreneurs panic that the world of opportunity is spiralling away from them at such a rate of knots that their customers will be gone by next year if they don't move fast. The fact is, for all of history the customers have lived without you and your business. They can wait a little longer. Your customers will still be there when you're ready.

The question now, is which market segment should you go for first? There are two key criteria to help you prioritise your market segments: these are *market growth* and *market access*.

Market growth

As you evaluate the four or five market segments you identified earlier, ask yourself, 'Is this market segment growing?' This is vital. Imagine you have two market segments. One of them is comprised of a lot of people but there are no new people entering the market segment. This is called a stagnant market. The other is a very, very small market segment but so many new people are entering it that it's doubling in size every year. This is called a fast growing market.

The number of people buying tablet computers is doubling every couple of months. All those people need protective cases for their expensive tablets and there are relatively few established competitors, making this a fast growing market.

On the other hand, consumers of fax machines are an example of a stagnant market. As people get ever-savvy with technology and email attachments, faxing is a dying art. I'd guess as many people leave the fax-machine market every year as join it. In addition, a good fax machine will last for a while just as the need to fax declines. The businesses that make fax machines are the big tech and electronics companies that have been in business for years. Deciding to compete for the fax machine market is almost certainly financial suicide for a startup because these large, entrenched, competitors have every possible advantage in production, sales and distribution.

The market segment with lots of people but no newbies is stagnant because whoever solved the problem before your business arrived has already saved the day and got a stranglehold. Fighting over the few new customers coming into that market segment is a fruitless battle, especially for the new rookie on the block (that's you). You're up against incumbents, meaning you'll have to tear a customer away from your competitor rather than win a new customer. In a stagnant market segment, whoever you're up against is most likely going to compete with fierce pricing and competitive jousting. You'll enter a league that's way beyond your skill level. It's a tough marketplace.

A growing market segment is far easier to win. And, beautifully, every business that supports that market will grow with it. The natural growth of the market segment will push your own business growth because new people entering the market segment will be looking for a solution and you'll be one of the few that provide it.

If the market segment is doubling in size, your business needs to be doubling in size every year just to keep up! To win this market hands down, you'll need to be increasing your market share over your competitors by growing even faster than the market is growing. Now there's a challenge! This is a great situation to be in because whatever happens, your business WILL grow in this scenario. Even a young player could get a foothold.

A growing market segment that is easy to access is better than just about any other market segment you could imagine. Even if the market segment is infinitesimally small, as a startup, you're still smaller. Imagine, there are two markets, market X and market Y. Market X may only be worth £10 million this year compared to market Y, which is worth a whopping £1 billion. But – here's the sanity check – at the moment your startup is worth nothing. If you grab 50% of the new market that's worth £10 million you'll still have a £5 million pound business. Happy days. If you grab nothing of the £1 billion pound marketplace – which is likely because you'll be lost among the noise of your competitors who are fiercely fighting over the morsels and shreds of the few new people entering the marketplace – your battle scars might prove fatal.

Once you have an established business, established customers, revenue and profit in the smaller, safer market that's doubling in size every year, there's nothing to stop you using some of the free cash you've spawned off from your successes to tap into the bigger market segment. Just don't get too greedy too soon.

Market access

The second criterion you can use to help you prioritise your market segment is market access. You'll want to target the fast growing market segment that is the easiest to reach.

The hardest challenge for a startup is marketing and that's because the startup is invisible. The web makes this situation more difficult. It puts everybody one foot (or click) away from you, teasingly, tantalisingly within your grasp but at the same time you're completely unknown and therefore invisible, floating around in the Internet ether. You have zero physical presence and the likelihood of people finding you just by chance is pretty slim.

Before the Internet, if you were on the high street a number of people would pound the pavement past your shop. The physicality of your shop front ensured that you had visibility. On the web, there's no 'passing by' your business. You're either visible, or you're not.

One of the reasons marketplaces on the web (like Amazon, eBay, Not On The High Street and our lovely friends at Folksy) have acquired power and value is that they've recreated or mimicked some of that 'passing by' on the high street, but online. They've created a path to visibility.

The way to think about the web is as buckets of places where customers already go, because we know there are millions of people – of customers – online. It becomes your job to *intercept*

the customer where they are already going, rather than try to persuade them to go somewhere else. You don't interrupt their experience with a pop-up advert, you intercept them on their way to their goal and you steer them to your website to quickly solve their problem or fulfil their desire.

If you need to choose between two fast-growing market segments, choose the market segment where you have more and easier access to potential customers. You want to minimize the time and money required to reach these revenue sources.

The story of the Shewee

www.shewee.com

A few years ago when I was on Dragons' Den, a woman came on the programme and introduced us to a Shewee, a portable urinating device to allow women to pee standing up.

She wanted to know whether she should sell it to one market segment, which was the recreational, backpacking, hiking, festival-going public or whether she should sell it to another market segment – the military – to be supplied to female soldiers.

This is a great illustration of the market segment question. The same product (the Shewee) had the potential to attract two completely

different market segments and those market segments had vastly different attributes: it was a face-off between the weekend hiker and the battle-zone fighter. To make the decision, the Shewee creator, Samantha, had to apply the selection criteria that we've explored above. She had to rate the market segments to decide which was the best one to go for. The decision-making process went like this:

Question. Market Growth: Was one of the market segments growing?
Answer. Yes, the recreational market segment.

Recreational market segment: 1
Military market segment: 0

Question. How accessible were the markets?
Answer. The military market would involve a sales cycle that could take one, two, maybe three years. The military market appeared from a distance to be huge but it wasn't a growth market. It had a group of hard-to-reach people who made all the decisions. The recreational market segment, on the other hand, had lots of different channels of distribution, both physical and via the web. It also had a growing population of people and was an easy market to reach.

Recreational market segment: 2
Military market segment: 0

It became obvious. That's why this analysis is useful; it gives you clear direction.

Sometimes defining the market segment actually changes your product or service. It transpired that the Shewee for retail or distribution to the recreational market would require packaging, which would cost money, possibly even as much money as the Shewee itself. The packaging would play such a key role in selling the product that it would actually become part of the product. It would influence the purchaser considering an impulse buy. It would be two-phase – the packaging of the product and the display packaging for retail. It would be designed to entice. It would vary by country as US stores and UK shops have different sales techniques and retail etiquette.

This might seem like a lot more work was required for the product to be ready for the recreational market segment. All that research and branding and design and packaging… and of course, the associated cost! If the Shewee were being sold to the military it would be transported in bulk not via retail, removing the need for packaging and cost and the headache that goes with it. But Samantha's customer in the recreational market is in the retail environment already, making it far easier to access directly and that's what matters most. In spite of the additional effort of branding and packaging, it still made good business sense to focus on the recreational market segment.

Now, of course, the Shewee has proven success and has been able to grow, to access those other market segments like the military. By starting small, the Shewee developed a solid market proposition and could steady itself and then grow into other markets.

VS

DIFFERENTIATING YOUR PRODUCT TO SELL MORE EFFECTIVELY TO YOUR TARGET MARKET SEGMENT

Whisky producers are particularly good at changing their products to meet the expectations of different market segments. A great case study is Johnnie Walker, a whisky manufacturer established in 1820 that has grown to include six different blends, each associated with a different coloured label.

Variations on the product are available under different guises as Johnnie Walker Red, Johnnie Walker Black, Johnnie Walker Double Black, Johnnie Walker Gold, Johnnie Walker Platinum and for the most discerning customers, the rare blend of Johnnie Walker Blue. A lot of the difference between products seems to be in the packaging and in variations in description. Terms like 'hand-crafted' and 'single-barrelled' help the customer to perceive six very different whisky blends on a scale of rising exclusivity and cost.

The supreme whisky – Johnnie Walker Blue – was, I believe, designed largely for the Asian market that wanted a more prestigious product and thus became a key market for Johnnie Walker. The whisky pioneers realised they were losing out by not having a super premium whisky in their blend lines for that market and so they added a Blue label to capture it.

What Johnnie Walker has done, probably more ably than anyone else in the world, is create variations of their product targeted at segments of the market. They've actually segmented the segment, slicing the market very thinly across one variable: *levels of wealth*.

Johnnie Walker has done a great job of creating a parent brand and has used the colour of the labels on their bottles to create micro-brands for each tiny segment. It's actually very elegant marketing. Everyone knows it's Johnnie Walker and yet each customer feels they are getting a version of Johnny Walker tailored just for them.

What this chapter is asking you to do is figure out who your market is (the orange), who your market segments are and then rate them by the criteria we've looked at above (size, growth, accessibility) so that you can work out your *priority* market segment. Now aim there.

STARTUP STORY: THE CUSTOMER

FLEUR EMERY

CO-FOUNDER, GRASSHOPPER

www.grasshopper-foods.com

Fleur Emery co-founded Grasshopper in 2005. The business originally sold instant porridge pots but developed its product line and its packaging in response to market trends. Grasshopper's willingness to respond to customer demand for innovation has resulted in the creation of unique and instantly recognisable packaging and an exponential increase in the value of the business as a whole. Grasshopper's customers have included Waitrose, The Soho House Group, Whole Foods, Ocado and MyHotels. Fleur has since co-founded an all-natural craft-brewed lager company, Green and Pleasant.

I was a Spanish literature graduate and my sister Abi's degrees were in science so we had no business education at all when we began. We literally worked it out as we went along. I had just spent a year playing poker for a living so it's fair to say that I was a natural risk-taker, in common with many entrepreneurs; Abi was more pragmatic about things and provided a natural brake to my boundless self-belief! One thing that we are both good at though is relationships. We both like people and are interested in other people's experiences and once we had the courage to really 'put it out there' and tell people what we were trying to do, we were overwhelmed by the help and support. Entrepreneurs are known to be ego-driven and I'm no exception – I like the sound of my own voice and I assume I know best, but to move forward that trait was something I had to overcome; I had to take the cotton wool out of my ears and put it in my mouth, as they say.

Abi and I come from a yachting family and had always spent a lot of time on or in the water off the south coast of England. At that time there was no way to make porridge portable so we came up with a solution ourselves and it caught on in the sailing community. Initially we made up the chopped oats, milk powder and dried fruit mix at home and made labels to stick on the pots ourselves. Our first customers were yachts in Hamble marina; we told people what we were doing and they emailed orders in. On race day they left their hatches open so that Abi could jump down into the galley, like a monkey, and leave their porridge. The business model at that time was no more developed than leaving flyers on windscreens.

Our product unwittingly satisfied retail's demand for innovation and our talent lay in creating a brand that people warmed to, so we won trophy customers such as Harvey Nichols early on. In fact we went from concept to Waitrose in 18 months, which is more or less unheard of. Getting a volume customer like Waitrose gave us breathing space to learn more about business and get help planning the business and funding it properly. By interacting with our customers at events and on the internet we realised that the product that we had originally made for sailing was appealing to a wide range of people who wanted something healthy but fun to eat while they were on the move. We had customers eating Grasshopper pots while they were doing all kinds of things, from translating for the United Nations to marching schoolboys along the Great Wall of China. I love that the internet was able to really put us in touch with all these people. It made the project feel creatively very rich for us, very meaningful.

Our products did well in the travel industry with clients like Eurostar, Air New Zealand and Virgin Trains. We also won 'Best Onboard Food' at the International Travel Catering Association awards, which is like the Oscars of airline food. The more we spoke to these customers the more we realised how much they wanted products that use up less storage space. We took that feedback on board and really started thinking about it. We were motivated to give our travel customers something different because several large corporate

companies had launched similar products to ours and we were starting to get pushed around, so we needed to redefine ourselves somehow. We knew the pot wasn't perfect so we decided to focus on improving it in a really dynamic way. After partnering with some great design talent we came up with the Grasshopper Hopper Pot. When our managing director presented the prototype, the atmosphere in the board-room changed and everyone started clapping. It was a breakthrough moment as we all recognised that the design was right in so many ways. We applied for multiple patents to protect everything about the new packaging and started presenting to customers, who loved it as much as we did.

As a company we invested a lot of time and money in finding this 'next step'. It was something that we were able to do because we had taken the time to re-finance and, to complement our own creativity, we sourced proven business acumen in the form of our venture capitalist partners. The packaging doesn't solve the challenges that we still face in retail with the market now dominated by corporate brands

but it gives us something really exciting to take to customers. They can see that we have listened to them and delivered something different. The most exciting part of this development, that I could have never foreseen when Abi and I were selling our porridge at Cowes Week, is how ownership of the Intellectual Property rights to our packaging designs has increased the value of Grasshopper as a business in a way that selling more porridge in Waitrose simply never could. It offers potential for a completely separate revenue stream in terms of licensing fees or a dramatically increased sale price if we were to sell the company. We are still very much enjoying life as a snack food company with porridge and soups selling well and noodles due soon but it's great to know that the company now has an added value that acts as a kind of insurance policy safeguarding the time and money that our family and friends invested.

NOW YOU KNOW...

- You now understand the difference between the market for your products, the market segments for your product, and the total available market for your products.
- You understand how knowing relevant characteristics about people who love your products can help you find more people like them.
- You understand why you need to pick a fast growing market segment to direct your efforts toward.

- You understand why you need to target a large available market for your product, specifically a group of people you can reach in large numbers for little or no cost.
- You understand that you define your product based on the buyer.
- You know you can vary your price, product and packaging to target different groups of people within a target market segment.

WHAT YOU'VE ACCOMPLISHED...

If you've followed the steps in this chapter you have:

- Assessed your target markets, reviewed your market segments, considered your total available market.
- Identified a fast growing market you can serve that you can reach quickly and cost effectively.
- Begun to review your product or service to ensure you can make it perfectly suit this tightly targeted market.

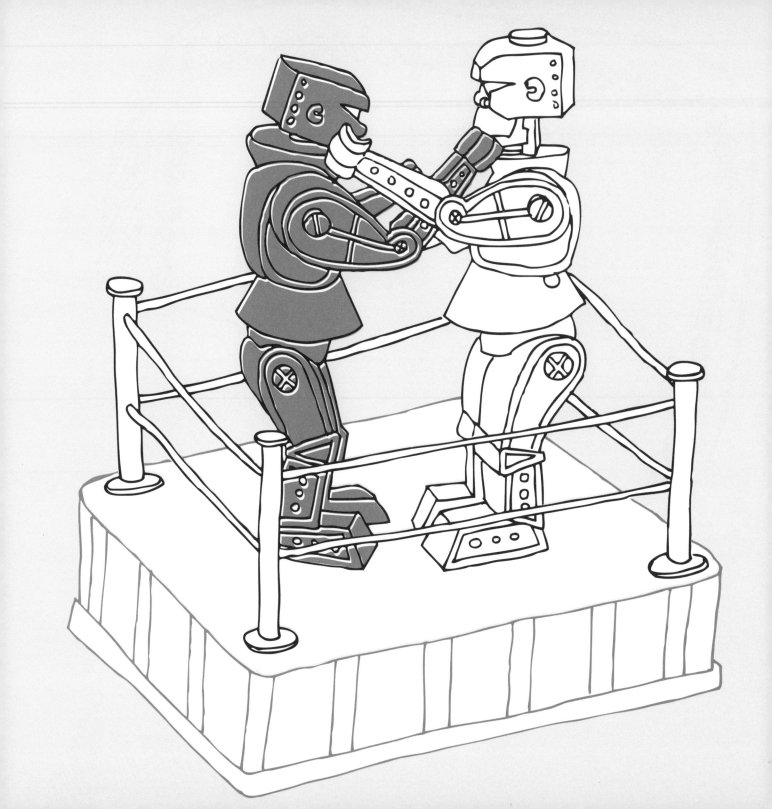

CHAPTER 3: THE COMPETITION

WHO ARE WE UP AGAINST?

WHO ARE WE UP AGAINST?

Once you know your proposition and the market segment you want to target, you can start sizing up your competition. Some companies compete worldwide, some nationally, some locally. Think about your market and its boundaries when you assess your competitors.

A little piece of advice: If your product or service is based on artistic endeavour, don't let the artisan in you overshadow your ability to see your competitors in the real, more mundane world. If you create beautiful, artistic lampshades, remember that they are, first and foremost, lampshades. Your competitors are other companies that produce lampshades, not other artists. Turning functional things into artistically enhanced functional things is wonderful but from a sales point of view, they are primarily functional things. If you think of your work as art, then all of your website language will categorise you in the internet search rankings as art – great for your profile as an artist, not so great for your business. All I'm saying is, you might have to swallow your pride and think of your business in a less creative way to see where it fits in the marketplace. This doesn't mean sacrificing your creative integrity, it just means you need to wear your business hat in some instances.

If you have a peek into the workings of your close competitors, you'll be surprised how many routes there are to contact your customers and close sales. You'll also uncover some useful marketing strategies and perhaps even some suppliers you can buy from in the future.

Watch your successful competitors to learn how to run a better, more profitable business. They'll have solved most of the problems you're facing. They know what your customers want and how to provide it. Your objective in studying them is to learn what they do well and then improve it with your own innovations.

Good business is about standing on the shoulders of giants. Who can you learn from? Whose expertise can you borrow? Who has done the hard graft and the research, so that you can pinch it (in an honest way, obviously) and use it to help your own business thrive?

To find customers and keep them, your product or service must offer advantages over those of your competitors. To deliver a better product or service than others do you must understand that there's a difference between a product's features and its advantages.

A product may come in red, green, blue or orange; these are features. A service may be delivered on weekdays, on weekends and on holidays; these are all features too. A feature may have no value at all to a given customer, because just being different doesn't make a product better. On the other hand, when a feature does have value to a customer it's because it delivers some advantage to them. For example, perhaps the colour matches their eyes or the size will make it look good in the kitchen, etc.

Dorset Cereals is an interesting example here. They came out with a package that was intentionally the wrong size – in terms of how we see it. They created a package that didn't fit the standard cereal box shape. It stood out on the cereal shelf because it was a skinny oblong. It looked out of place. It caught the eye of the consumer. There is a huge amount of research that goes into consumer behaviour in a supermarket because of the lucrative nature of food retail. Research says that customers don't look up or down on entering the supermarket, they look straight in front of them and their line of sight varies by only 5–10 degrees. Research says customers notice strap lines and the unexpected.

The success of Dorset Cereals, I would argue, is founded on the weird shape of the package. Maybe repeat customers buy it because they love the contents (the cereal) but they couldn't have known they would love it on that very first purchase. There was a reason they picked that box off the shelf and that was because of the unusual packaging. That package was a *feature* of the product.

Since Dorset Cereals got oh-so-clever with their packaging, there are now all sorts of inventive ways to package cereals. It makes little difference of course, because there is no longer a wall of generic cereal boxes to stand out against. Difference has become the norm. The feature of the cereal box shape didn't provide an advantage to the Dorset Cereals customer but it sure got the brand noticed.

FEATURES AND ADVANTAGES

Understanding the difference between features and *advantages* is critical because startups don't have the funding required to match competing products and services feature by feature. Instead they must deliver products with few features that deliver great advantage to their customers.

A small custom wedding dress designer in South London can't offer brides the full range of gowns delivered by Vera Wang. What this designer can offer is the advantage of a unique gown, custom fit, in the fabric of the bride's choice within the budget she can afford. Those advantages are what the designer needs to promote because she can't compete on the basis of reputation.

In the following pages you'll find a list of advantages your product may deliver better than its competitors. You'll deliver at least one meaningful advantage to your customers already or they'd have no reason to buy what you sell. Just like our Ten Questions, not all advantages are equally weighted.

New advantage

Let's start with an overused and unimpressive advantage: New. My least favourite phrase in marketing is 'new and improved' because that's impossible. If it's new, then it's not improved! I think those marketers need to choose one or the other.

'New' means that your product depends upon newness. Take the fashion industry, where new means there is pressure to produce the new range, a new season's selection. The challenge of 'new' is that it's a tyranny. If the only thing that provides your product advantage is that it's 'new' and you've just created it, then you're tied to the hamster wheel to keep producing new items forevermore. It's relentless, because you must always be producing. New is therefore a lesser advantage. It takes a lot of work to maintain over time.

Successful fashion labels don't just have new lines, they have staples. Why? Because those staples are the cash cow that they can continue to milk. People buy the perennial not the annual. They buy the staples. The new range that comes out seasonally is about promoting the fashion brand whilst the staples keep the cash tills ringing.

PERFORMANCE ADVANTAGE

Performance becomes an advantage when you are explicitly saying that your product moves faster, does more, or does it better. Lots of things are sold on performance. For many years computers were sold on performance. Cars can be sold on the fact that they do more miles to the gallon which is a form of performance. Performance is usually a measurable advantage; it's literally based on how the product or service performs.

The notion of performance usually means somebody has something and you're selling them a better version, so most companies that have performance as a main advantage are competing directly with another company.

Remember, though, that to snatch customers from your competitor, it's not enough for your product or service to perform better than the competitor, it has to perform better than the competitor, *plus the cost and hassle of switching to you*. Put yourself in your customer's shoes and ask yourself, is the switch from a competitor to you worth the cost and the hassle?

Performance can work at the time of natural purchase where the business can boast, 'We're better than they are' or 'We're cheaper than they are' or 'We're faster than they are'. The performance advantage can also be a benefit felt over time.

An example: A big challenge for people who make boilers is that nobody ever replaces a working boiler. Why? Because they're expensive. Why would you buy a new boiler if your current boiler still works? Well, recently in the UK our energy prices have been hiked so high that it's finally become more cost effective to replace a boiler that does the job, with a new boiler that's more energy efficient. The money saved on bills gives the new boiler a *performance advantage*. The benefit to the customer is felt over time (through savings on their energy bills) but the cost of switching also has to be taken into account. This is an *investment advantage* meaning that the customer buys now and reaps the benefits later. As a rule, people don't like to make their money later; they don't want to wait to earn the reward. The investment advantage is therefore a hard sell.

PRICE ADVANTAGE

People get pricing wrong all the time. When it comes to competing on price, every competitor falls in one of these three camps:

1) Cheapest
2) Most expensive
3) Value for money

Most products fall into the third camp – value for money – meaning simply that the customer will get more for their money.

In all likelihood, as a startup you won't be able to sell the same products, using components from the same suppliers, through the same channels for a lower price than your competitors. You'll go out of business trying. Big companies can offer lower prices because they can get better rates from suppliers, distributors and sales channels. A young business should never make lowest price their chief advantage. The only exception would be if you've found a brand new way to deliver a product or service that is amazingly, blindingly, less expensive to produce, market and sell. That's quite rare.

If you're the cheapest on the market it means you need to be running a cheaper business than your competitors, so every single one of your business costs needs to be consistently lower than your competition. That's hard. You'll struggle to keep being the cheapest over the long term. Sometimes all you achieve by dropping your price is to offer a better deal to your current customer and you don't win any new customers.

What does all this mean? It means your product has to find *other* advantages instead of lowest price. It won't be the cheapest product or service on the market but depending on the product or service you offer, it could be the best fitting, or the fastest or most luxurious. It could be the softest, the most responsive or the easiest to customise. Maybe it's the best product for a specific niche of customers. Creative startups should never compete only on the basis of price, but on the

basis of value. Provide a better product or service, delivered at a price the customer is willing to pay. Despite what you may think, customers will pay a premium for a product or service that offers great value.

Canny businesses that can offer the lowest price often do so along with some additional benefit. One of the most successful chains in the UK is Tesco. Tesco offer the cheapest food but they also have a large selection of food. They have cheap prices *and* availability of stock. One of the most interesting companies in the world right now is Amazon. Like Tesco, they don't merely have a price selection. They have a decent price and a good selection of stock. They have price *and* availability. It's insanely easy to shop at Amazon. They might not be the absolute cheapest but they are the cheapest option if you want the product *right now*.

SHARED OWNERSHIP ADVANTAGE

Under this model, a business allows people to share ownership of an item or location. Warren Buffett, world-renowned billionaire, bought a company called NetJets that was essentially a fleet of jets and offered people with a large stack of cash (let's call them millionaires) the chance to share ownership of a jet. Those who could afford the NetJets fee could show up at any airfield in the world and a jet would take them wherever they wanted to go. The wealthy customer was buying shared access, a share of ownership in a very expensive item (a jet). A few years ago that might have been the only example I could use for shared access ownership, but now there is all sorts of innovation in the shared ownership or *access* model. Zipcar (www.zipcar.com) is the company that bought Streetcar and provides shared access to cars. Zipcar can be found in dense urban cities where there is a high population of people and not a lot of parking space. They have removed the headache and expense of car ownership as they claim that there's always a Zipcar ready for use a couple of streets away from any customer. They've got the edge on the rental car market because with rental cars the minimum unit of rental is a day and for Zipcar it's an hour.

PERSONALISATION ADVANTAGE

This is where you sell something and layer a personalised element on top to differentiate it. Take the men's suit company, A Suit That Fits (www.asuitthatfits.com). They've hit a double whammy of personalisation *and* driving down the price; they've moved into the value position. A Suit That Fits make made-to-measure suits that cost the same price as a men's off-the-rack suit from one of the big suit labels (and for the uninitiated, a made-to-measure suit falls somewhere between bespoke and off-the-rack). We're talking a suit made in the same high quality material, tailored to the individual and sold at a cost to rival a suit pulled off the hanger in a high-end designer store. A Suit That Fits have personalised the service and made it affordable, so much so that the customer has to ask themselves, why wouldn't they want a tailor-made suit over a shop-bought standard?

DESIGN ADVANTAGE

This is an obvious one. Design is a differentiator and an advantage. A product that is beautiful stands apart in its own right. I have always desired beauty in all of the products that my companies made. Sadly, some people don't see the value in design at all but if you get it right, great design is a business advantage.

BRAND ADVANTAGE

A brand is not a logo or a product. A brand is the emotion that is left behind after the product is gone. A brand is the desire to belong. A brand is largely a promise.

A brand is what you think in your mind when you order a branded drink, like a Jack Daniel's and Coke, rather than a whisky and cola. Consciously or not, stating a preference for one brand over another is making a statement about yourself.

Many years ago, Pepsi-Cola, the perennial second choice the world over and insecure down to its bones about being second choice the world over, was delighted to find out that on a blind tasting, people actually preferred Pepsi, to Coke. They brought this news to the world via the Pepsi Challenge – a campaign that has been running since 1975. Unfortunately for Pepsi, people don't

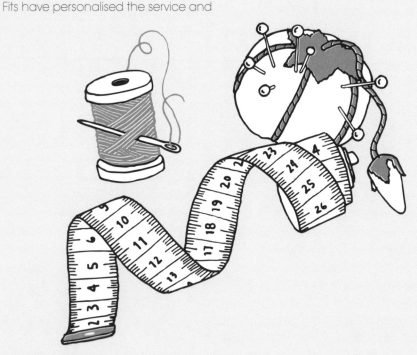

drink their Pepsi or Coke blindfolded. This revelation from the Pepsi Challenge didn't translate into increased sales of Pepsi. If people think that they prefer Coke and they see themselves as a Coke drinker, then even on the evidence from a blind tasting, they'll still go to the supermarket and buy Coke. The power of a brand is that it can actually change the consumer's taste.

There is an entire area of cognitive psychology that talks about how we define our own identities by the views others have of us. We see ourselves reflected in the eyes of people who judge us. We are deeply social beings shaped by the perceptions of others. If you can become a company that influences how others perceive themselves you have firstly, become a brand and secondly, you have a brand advantage. When you're competing against a branded product you're competing against the perception they've created in the marketplace that sets them apart.

As a young company you should be aware that it's really difficult to grow a brand. You need to start out with a very clear view of your brand so that *everything* you do from the beginning of your business journey supports your brand.

RISK REDUCTION

This is the kind of advantage you throw into the mix when the act of purchasing from you is a risk in its own right. A great example here is used cars. There is a risk in buying a used car because you're never quite sure what you're buying. Mercedes invented a new term for their used cars and you can now flick through the car classified ads and find something called a 'pre-owned' Mercedes. Mercedes have renamed their used cars 'pre-owned' and, because the Mercedes brand is so strong, consumers are more trusting of this proposition. Mercedes will even provide a warranty on the re-purchased car, which diminishes the risk to the customer. It's an advantage that offsets the risk.

JARGON BUSTER!

Remarkability is about creating something so remarkable that people talk about how very remarkable it is.

REMARKABILITY

This is the ease with which one customer can connect you to another and the incentive you offer them to make that connection. This is marketing mogul Seth Godin's gem of a term. It captures the concept perfectly so I've borrowed it here.

The key to all marketing is word of mouth. Your single most important goal in marketing is to create word of mouth about your company and what you sell. We are inherently social animals and we often look to the people around us to tell us what we should do, think, wear, and buy.

Skype is a *remarkable* product because using the product requires a customer to tell those people that they want to Skype with to use the product as well. Facebook and Twitter work exactly the same way. Nike shoes, Gucci bags and Rolex watches are all marketed in a similar fashion. People who wear them are promoting the brand just by wearing them, because their branding is so distinctive.

Sometimes a product creates its own word of mouth. Apple products don't provide more features than their competitors but they are more likeable products. They are beautifully designed, sleek, aspirational products. They are made to be shown off. They all but sell themselves.

Business advantage

You can create advantages for customers in how you run your business. For example, you could be trustworthy and responsive in an industry where most of your competitors simply never answer the phone. Alternatively, if you're able to take on challenges artistically or commercially that your competitors won't touch, that's a business advantage as well.

You can have a business that sells exactly the same product that everyone else sells and yet earns far more just because your business does a better job of ensuring the customer will be happy with their purchase.

A great example of how the business model can flip an entire industry, starts with the video rental chain Blockbuster Video. Blockbuster had video shops on the high street where you walked in, picked up a VHS or a DVD and took it home to watch. Or at least, you aspired to watch it. Typically, life took over. You forgot you had dinner plans, a friend popped by, your Mum called, the kids were doing their homework… and you didn't get to watch the film. Days passed. The film sat on the table with your car keys, waiting to be returned. You returned it late and you got fined a late fee. That was frustrating. Renting from Blockbuster became a tension-inducing financial relationship. Time passed while the tape languished on the table increasing the urgency and

the annoyance that you should watch the film or return it, neither of which came to pass.

In the US, a new startup on the block – Netflix – changed the business model. With Netflix, you could rent the same video or DVD as you could at Blockbuster but it would be delivered directly to your door and better yet, there was no late fee! No pressure, no urgency, no tension-inducing financial relationship. It was exactly the same product but with no monetary fine which was the one itch that drove people crazy about Blockbuster. Blockbuster is now bankrupt. Netflix is worth billions of dollars in value. What Netflix did was change the pricing model. That was the only change they made. In the UK the equivalent has been LoveFilm and later in the book we're lucky enough to hear from Saul Klein who owned one of the three companies that merged to become LoveFilm.

The advantage that Netflix and LoveFilm offered the customer, in removing a late fee, developed into a benefit. Customers were saying, 'I prefer to use this company (rather than Blockbuster) because I can benefit.'

ETHICAL OR SOCIAL GOOD ADVANTAGE

More and more customers are supporting businesses that align with their notions of social justice and ethical business practice. This is, in general, a good advantage to have.

Your business can be socially conscious, ethically conscious,

environmentally conscious or a social enterprise but I say this to my students all the time: *You cannot do good until you have done well.*

The path to doing good through business is through doing well because a business that doesn't do well goes broke and can no longer do good! Part of your business mission may be to drive awareness about a social issue or a common good but people must buy the product or service that you offer first. The social message gets carried with the success of the brand.

You don't need to brush aside your ethical credentials but do make sure you build a viable business platform on which to express them. A social enterprise must be an enterprise first and foremost. The social bit comes second.

CUSTOMER SERVICE ADVANTAGE

Getting customer service right is one of the easiest and most important things you can do to become more successful. Good service increases customer satisfaction, encourages follow-on sales from happy customers, and it vastly increases referrals of your business to new customers. Many enterprises spend a great deal of time and effort acquiring new customers but very few resources in keeping them, which is just crazy. Existing customers have already proven that they can – and will – buy from you and you already know exactly where to find them.

Amazon – my current favourite – wants every call from a customer to become simply the best customer support experience the customer has ever had. They sidestep customer support problems by making ordering online easy; they provide ways to track what may go missing; they make it easy to report failed deliveries and to return products. They don't quibble and they put the customer first. Amazon has turned customer service into an advantage.

ALL THE ADVANTAGES YOU'VE JUST LEARNED ABOUT ARE EMOTIONAL ADVANTAGES

Advantages are based on emotions. The next time you go shopping, pay attention to what you think and feel as you put each item in your shopping basket. You might buy a brand of toothpaste because it promises you white teeth. You are probably thinking of how embarrassed you'll be if your teeth are discoloured. You might buy a brand of jam because your Nan used to buy it and buying it reminds you of her. Everything, from aeroplanes to air freshener, is purchased because the customer felt an emotion, however small, that made them 'pull the trigger' on the purchase.

Never make the mistake of thinking that people buy for rational reasons. There are all kinds of good reasons to buy things we ought to buy and never do and it is because we are not emotionally driven to purchase them.

Companies build strong brands by understanding the emotional advantages that compel their customers to purchase what they sell. They ensure every aspect of their product, service, support sales and marketing strengthens those emotional associations.

ADVANTAGES SUMMARY

Your product's value in any given sales environment is based on:

1. The advantages your customers believe your product, service or business offers.
2. Your product's cost to the customer measured in money, in effort and in risk.
3. The advantages and prices of available competing products or services.

As a young startup pup making your way in the world, you need to consciously collect advantages in your product, service or business model that your tightly defined, fast-growing target market will value.

- Advantages are emotion-based. Individual products and services may appeal to customers who want to feel safer, more in control, more connected to others or just plain amused.
- Your product or service does not have to match competing products feature for feature in order to be successful.
- Your product or service does have to deliver advantages that customers want.
- Your product or service must, eventually, be priced so that the advantages you provide are good value relative to the price you charge.
- Your business must learn how to find and contact customers who will value the bundle of advantages you sell.

GET YOUR HANDS DIRTY

Try this: List the advantages your product or service delivers in the context of its competitors.

- List the features of your product.
- List the advantages your product delivers to customers.
- List the emotions associated with each advantage.

- How does your product make people safer?
- How does it give them more control?
- How does it expose them to experiences that they like?
- How does it help them feel that they belong?
- As you begin to sell your product, collect customer quotes and testimonials where people discuss the advantages your product delivers.
- Keep the emotional benefits associated with each advantage in mind when creating the content that will market what you sell. List the features of your product.

Mapping your product's advantages to the emotions that make people buy it.

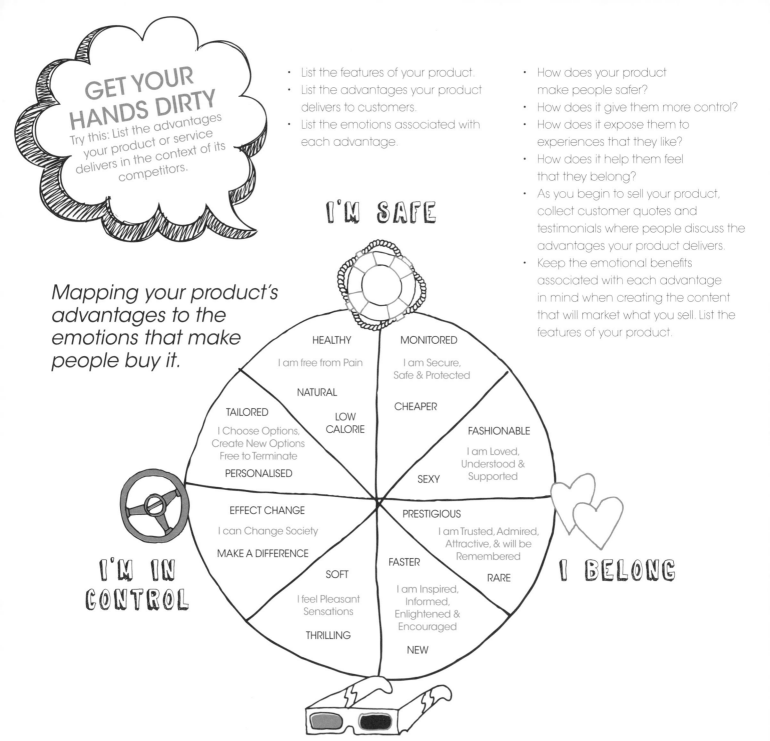

I'M SAFE

HEALTHY
I am free from Pain
NATURAL
LOW CALORIE

MONITORED
I am Secure, Safe & Protected
CHEAPER

TAILORED
I Choose Options, Create New Options Free to Terminate
PERSONALISED

FASHIONABLE
I am Loved, Understood & Supported
SEXY

EFFECT CHANGE
I can Change Society
MAKE A DIFFERENCE

PRESTIGIOUS
I am Trusted, Admired, Attractive, & will be Remembered
FASTER
RARE

SOFT
I feel Pleasant Sensations
THRILLING

I am Inspired, Informed, Enlightened & Encouraged
NEW

I'M IN CONTROL

I BELONG

I'M ENTERTAINED

Find out how your product can sell and resell itself through 'remarkability'

Take time to think about how you can adjust your product or service so it practically sells itself. How can you ensure that everyone who buys or sees your product will know who made it and where they can buy one?

If you deliver your products to people via snail mail, ask for a delivery email address so you can let those receiving gifts know when a product is scheduled to arrive. If you deliver a service to customers, allow them to 'gift' the service to new customers either for free or at a deep discount.

Identify and assess your competition

- Create a list of products and services that your competitors sell to your tightly defined, fast-growing, easily-accessible target market.
- Now think more broadly and include on your list companies that produce products and services that meet the same need or desire as your products do.
- Now write down the proposition (from Chapter 1) for each of your competitors. What problem have they solved or what desire have they fulfilled?
- For each competing product or service, identify the top three or four advantages that drive people to buy this particular product or service. You'll find online customer reviews very helpful in working out how people value your competitors and make their consumer choices.
- Next to each product, record the advantages each offers to the customer.
- Note where the product or service is sold. Did you find it online? Can you buy it online?
- Record the price of each product or service including the variances you see, based on where it is sold.

Record this information in a spreadsheet for future reference. You'll be returning to it often as you work through the rest of this book. Look at the data you collected about your competitors:

- What promises do your competitors make to their customers?
- Where do they find their customers?
- What marketing methods do they use?
- How do they deliver their product or service to their customers?
- How do they price their product online, offline, through resellers and through third parties?
- What key marketing partners do they have?
- Where do they find suppliers?
- Where do they recruit employees?

Now identify the unique advantages that your products, services and business offer your customers.

COMPETITOR SPREADSHEET

	ADVANTAGES	CAN BE PURCHASED AT	PRICE RANGES	NOTES / THOUGHTS
LONDON BABIES *"Easy wash blankets in bright colours"*	Easy to wash Bright/Circus colors Ineresting patterns Cheap London Imagery	Etsy.com LondonBabies.com Popups Markets around London	£ 50⁰⁰ 100⁰⁰ 150⁰⁰	Baby baskets a good idea Do I want to sell cheap stuff? Customers come from Google I think
PIGGLE WIGGLE FINE BABIES *"All natural bedding for babies we love"*	Organic Sturdy Original/hand drawn art Heirloom/Handed Down	PiggleWiggleBaby.com High Street Boutiques	£ 200⁰⁰ 300⁰⁰	Really expensive/nice Seem to be selling a lot Targeting very high end People see in stores then buy I think.
BATTERSEA KIDS *"Like grandma used to make"*	Knitted/Handmade Llama wool Washable/Durable Hypoallergenic?	BatterseaKids.co.uk Amazon	£ 100⁰⁰ 200⁰⁰ 300⁰⁰	Really expensive Sell well online Amazon has lowest price. Sell mostly on Amazon?
KANGA-ROO BABY WEAR *"Cuddly clothes for little ones"*	Llama wool & soft canvas Interesting Pocket Design Very soft	Kanga-Roo-Clothes.com	£ 150⁰⁰ 250⁰⁰	What's up with Llama? Maybe sell more than a blanket? High-end pricing seems to work. I like their kid coats. Maybe add? These guys ONLY sell online.

MY COMPANY ————

	ADVANTAGES	CAN BE PURCHASED AT	PRICE RANGES	NOTES / THOUGHTS
LAMB CAKES WOOL BLANKETS *"Warm wraps for your little lamb"*	Organic Made in the UK Very Soft Durable Washable Classic English Artwork	LambCakes.co.uk Baby shops in expenensive areas	£ 150⁰⁰ 200⁰⁰ 300⁰⁰	Sell on consignment to hi-end shops Make sure product labels point to site

STARTUP STORY: COMPETITION

JAMES BOARDWELL
CO-FOUNDER, FOLKSY
www.folksy.com

James Boardwell and Rob Lee came together to build Folksy after being inspired by the energy in the craft communities in the UK as well as North America and Australia. At the time they were developing Folksy, the web began offering ways to crowd-source solutions to problems and they were able to capitalise on this technological innovation. Folksy was created with the aim of showcasing the work of UK designers and makers. The site has since risen to become the most popular UK site for handmade gifts and supplies.

The idea for Folksy began in early 2000 in the grassroots, craft blogging movement but gathered momentum when Rob and I were researching ways to support people in the UK who were designing and making their own products. By 2006 Etsy had started in the US, although it was more or less unknown in the UK, and we spotted a big market for crafts and the rising popularity of handcrafted goods and the 'stitch and bitch' phenomenon.

Folksy was created as a platform to gauge the appetite for craft in the UK. A simple service was built over a few months in mid 2007. But it wasn't until 2008 that we launched Folksy in beta (remember those?) when we had some funds and time to spend on it.

A community of artists and crafters gravitated quickly to the platform and became an integral part of it, taking ownership of it and helping us to promote it. They loved that there was this new portal that celebrated the artisan of the homemade and that felt very 'social' in the days before web 2.0 had become popularised. The heartland of our community were the blogger-makers; those who were familiar with online publishing tools, though they were quickly joined by others eager to find out about Folksy.

Our original ethos for Folksy was very much as a place to share craft ideas and not just a place to sell. This carried over into the design and the core navigation was 'making, buying, selling, talking', which might seem strange but the talking aspect – the community – had come so quickly to define Folksy. We were great at listening, we were very human. Between 2009 and 2011 though, things began to shift and we had to choose between conflicting paths and audiences. Were we a showcase or a marketplace? We made some changes to the site in November 2011 based on feedback about becoming a more professional platform for craftspeople; a place that artists and designer-makers would feel did justice to their work. Some of the community felt alienated by the changes. We'd transformed Folksy from a showcase of handmade crafts to an active marketplace, an open service where anyone could sell their crafts and where new talent could be discovered. We really wanted to celebrate the skills, the learning and craftsmanship that define beautiful objects. The transition was a huge learning experience.

Our community now, although still mixed, is significantly craftspeople who are ambitious and are driven by the practical need to sell their creations and earn a living.

Our next step was to decide how to compete with the rising trend for boutique craft sellers online and with our overseas counterpart who was now making waves in the UK: Etsy. In some ways Folksy became defined by its humble beginnings and community of followers. Everyone loves the little man and you could say we are David to Etsy's Goliath! We really believed in the marketplace; Folksy is now a better platform for craft and we've become better at selling.

We have a lot of respect for Etsy, especially their technical team.. Ultimately Etsy helped to open up the market for craft, educating people about the value of things that have been handmade. Without Etsy, our job would have been much more difficult and they're a good competitor to have. But we want to develop independently, without playing catch up to others. We have a strong ethos, based on developing a social platform for designer makers to showcase their creativity and sell their work.

Folksy offers something different and we've held true to our values and what we believe in. We want to create a simpler platform. That, plus our size and the fact that we are focused on a smaller market – currently the UK and Northern Ireland although we are looking at reaching into Europe! – has helped us find our niche. We might be a small team without huge resource but being a nimble unit has great benefits; it means we're flexible and able to implement changes fast. We can benefit from seeing trends appearing in the market and swiftly acting on them. We don't have the mighty power or the huge budgets to make sweeping

changes or grand innovations but being agile has been a great asset. We also distinguish Folksy by its content; we're about showcasing craft talent and we've chosen to sidestep certain handmade themes such as vintage, which just aren't Folksy's thing.

We're always on the lookout for new innovation and new paths. Business is an iterative process and it's important that we keep exploring the possibilities so that Folksy continues to evolve, is relevant and can compete in the marketplace. As a company we're curious about how other online companies are run and how they're innovating. Pinterest and Facebook's 'gifting' are recent innovations that have got our attention. We don't set out to follow people – we wouldn't be true to ourselves and would lose our community if we did – but we have learned from our competitors' successes and their mistakes.

The challenge now is that of any burgeoning business: how do you maintain the small, cosy feel and familiar voice of a friendly startup, once you grow? We make changes that we think will help our craftspeople to sell their work more effectively. Involving them in the process of change is the big lesson we learnt from 2011. If we haven't told them where we're going or why, they aren't with us. We need to keep talking to our customers and get their feedback on our plans.

Last year we launched the 'Inspiration' piece, where craftspeople can tell their stories about how the item

was made and what inspired them. It's a compelling aspect because it connects the customer to the product through storytelling and emotion something we have found buyers, in particular, love. About 25% of our craftspeople use the facility and it has the power to really help them sell their work.

Going forward we're focusing on supporting a range of more social activities and, in many ways, developing the ethos we started with - allowing people to showcase work and have 'social' as core to the service, rather than as an add on. We've already moved in this direction, with the homepage themes now curated by our designer makers using Pinterest and also by showcasing newly listed work and bestsellers. There's more to come, in particular with integrating services like GoGoMargo that allow people to share their offline exhibitions and events where they're selling their wares.

There are a growing number of e-commerce platforms and a rising tide in craft appreciation and we'll work hard to continue our mission to be a great place for creative people to showcase and sell work.

NOW YOU KNOW...

- You now know why you don't have to compete feature-by-feature with existing products. What's important are the advantages you offer your customer, not the features of your product.
- You understand that all advantages are emotional. Only emotions make someone take out their wallet and buy something.
- You know that advantages don't just come from product features. How you accept payment for what you sell can deliver advantages to customers.
- You see why every product should be remarkable. The very act of purchasing it, or using it, should somehow connect the product to others who may want to buy it.

WHAT YOU'VE ACCOMPLISHED...

By following the steps in this chapter...

- You've assessed your product and the advantages it offers, and could offer in the future.
- You've analysed your competition, the advantages they offer your target market, and their price.
- You should now be able to see, based on the advantages you offer and the competition you face, how your product must be priced in order to be 'good value'.
- You've listed several ways you can make your product 'remarkable'.
- You can now describe, clearly: your product, its benefit, its purpose, its natural position in the market, who it's for, how they benefit, the segments in the market, which group of your customers is growing the most, and which is easiest to access.

With those answers, you'll be able to comfortably withstand any grilling on your business. Any question you're asked will lead to an answer that you've already banked from the previous three chapters. Put the kettle on. You've earned it.

CHAPTER 4: THE INDUSTRY

WHAT DO WE HAVE IN COMMON?

WHAT DO WE HAVE IN COMMON?

You have a lot in common with your competition and you can be sure that any trend that impacts them, or any underlying economic realities (like, say, a recession) that affect your competitors, will also impact you.

On the plus side, if the economic realities are positive and you're entering a fast-growing market, then even a mediocre product can generate tremendous wealth for its owners. The first version of the Google search engine was nowhere near as sophisticated as it is now, but being the only one available provided enough value that Google was able to grow along with its market. This was true of Amazon and eBay as well.

All things being equal, you should build your company to meet the needs of a fast-growing population of people who want a given product or service. The only caveat is that these people should also have the money or resources to pay for what you sell. In a recession there may be millions unemployed, so designing a product or service for this population will only make good financial sense if they can afford to buy what you sell, or if some other organisation or government agency is willing to pay for them to have it.

One of the best reasons to study the market trends, laws and taxes that impact you and your competitors is that you can find significant areas of opportunity and new business by meeting needs others haven't yet met.

If you're running a restaurant and your research on your industry indicates that most people are looking for organic meals, both vegetarian and sustainably sourced meat dishes, you can start doing the research to determine whether or not you'd get more customers and higher-paying customers for designing your restaurant to meet that need in your area first.

Any disruption in a market, no matter how it comes about, creates an opportunity for entrepreneurs who can meet those new needs. Even trends that would seem to be damaging to your industry can turn out to be beneficial. The decline of the print publishing industry might make anyone starting a magazine company appear insane but many would-be publishers are working with a collective of sponsors on a bespoke basis to create publications distributed by the sponsors to their customer base. Sites like Createspace.com and Lulu.com make that kind of custom publishing easy.

GET YOUR HANDS DIRTY
Try this: Find out which trends are impacting your industry.

Read trade publications that are written for your industry or profession. They'll give you a good indication of current trends. What problem seems to be addressed repeatedly? Does your product or service sidestep this issue? If you want to sell jewellery, problems with forgeries of precious gems in the jewellery business might be an industry problem on your radar. How does your product solve that problem? Does it provide an option for customisation that your competitors can't match? Is there something about your work that makes it so distinct, people will come to your site to find legitimate manufacturers?

EYE UP YOUR MOST SUCCESSFUL COMPETITION AND WRITE DOWN THE TRENDS THEY SEEM TO BE FOLLOWING

Your largest competitors often have better insight than you into how markets are shifting. They have more resources to throw at the problem. They might have a whole team of interns who are beavering away on market analysis and consumer behaviour. Luckily for a startup, the bigger companies are more cumbersome to manoeuvre. Changing the business model when you're a big business means the business has to crawl through many more layers of scrutiny and sign-off than a startup and that's where the startup can be nimble and light-footed. If you're a winemaker competing with bigger companies, you might spot organic wines as a popular trend and, being small, you're in a position to make all your wines organic. This is something the larger vineyards will not be able to do as quickly and it means you can capture a growing market that they currently can't serve.

A final word, just a nudge

There are some businesses that would be very easy to start and very profitable to run but for the legal requirements that make launching and running them all but impossible. Make sure you know what those costs are before you start the business and know what pending legislation might make things harder for you, before you begin. Are there any government regulations or licensing requirements that will impact your business?

For example, many customers value the word 'organic' but there are a great number of laws worldwide that govern when you can use that term on your products – and more legislation is pending. Make sure you know when and where you can use that term so you don't find yourself in trouble with some regulatory body.

STARTUP STORY: COMMONALITY

MIKE SMITH
PRESIDENT OF MUSIC, UNIVERSAL MUSIC
www.umusic.co.uk

Mike Smith has over twenty years' experience in the music industry, progressing from talent scout to Senior Vice President/Director of A&R at EMI, where he signed the likes of Supergrass, Arctic Monkeys, Kasabian and Blur. He spent six years as Managing Director at Sony Music's Columbia Records, signing artists such as Calvin Harris and The Vaccines to the Sony label. In September 2012 he joined Universal's Mercury division as President of Music.

The A&R (artists and repertoire) team is the talent sourcing team. They find the artist. They make the record. They are the research and development side of the business. Without them you don't have a product to sell. The A&R people are the ones who go out and find the artists, make the records with them and stay involved to make sure the record is as good as possible before it goes to market. The rest of the label is responsible for marketing and promoting the record, and promotion could take the form of radio promotion, TV and online. You've also got the sales team to take the goods to your customers. Customers traditionally were looked upon as retailers. Now we sell direct to the customer from the label's own website. There's also a brand partnerships division within the label because that's now a huge part of our business. There's ancillary income because we don't earn money just from record sales, we earn money from live shows, from tickets, from merchandise and brand sponsorship.

Within each of these departments we have younger people. Certainly within A&R we have talent scouts to keep us aware of everything that's going on, on the street. But also, by being the youngest and the sharpest and the most ambitious people within the department, they're responsible for filling us in on all the latest developments. To be a good executive and employee within a label you need to be aware of everything that's going on around you. You need to be reading all the relevant magazines, looking at what's going on online, conscious of the changes within the industry and how that affects you. We rely on having bright young people filling us in on their experiences and how they're consuming. I'm an avid music consumer and I try and consume it in every possible way so that I get a full sense of what our customers want. It's pretty tough if you can't identify with your customer.

The old generation of record stores are going under and that's happening to other industries too, like computer shops. There is a place for the new record shops but they need to be bookshops and coffee shops as well. They need to be a place where you go and hang out and listen to music – more of a social hub. That's true of all retail experiences I guess. They should be places where you can eat, drink, sample the merchandise, hang out and meet like-minded people. The notion of a place where you just go and buy records is long gone.

The record business was appallingly castigated by the media for being slow to react to the digital age and the irony is that the music business in many ways has reacted better and faster than the print world has. The problems that beset the music industry are basically besetting anyone that creates content these days. Journalists have experienced karma to some extent, in that the physical newspaper is now largely as redundant as the compact disc or vinyl record. Music journalism still has an important role to play but that's as much about blogs as the printed paper. The *NME* has a circulation which is a fraction of what it used to be but the online *NME* is thriving.

It is a fair comment that the music industry was slow to respond to online and I think we were all desperately clinging to the old business model and inevitably didn't want that to change. But having guys in their fifties and sixties running the business probably didn't make for the most receptive, innovative business decisions at that time. Now the industry is run by fresher, more astute individuals. The industry has become more professional because there is a lot less money around. It's a more efficient industry, it's more research driven than gut instinct. In the old days you could put an album together for a lot less money and allow the artist to develop over their second and third albums. Nowadays budgets are much tighter, so a lot of money goes on the first record. If the first record doesn't work, it's too expensive to roll the dice and make a second or third album. The digital age has enabled us to research things more thoroughly. We know immediately if people are looking at a band or interested in a band, how many views their videos have had, how many followers they have on the social networks. It's a lot more grown-up and serious.

Since the development of the web, it's been a lot easier for people to get hold of music and for people to get a hold of me. It's very easy for someone to get an email in front of me. It doesn't mean I'll respond any differently to days when I received letters rather than emails but those contacting me now are more creative; the way in which people contact me and how they contact me has changed.

I'm constantly going out and talking to new people. It's about never being afraid to embrace change and I think, unfortunately, when business is confronted by change it tends to stop it and try to crush it. The music industry did that with Napster. Napster was an illegal file-sharing service bought by BMG, so a record company was suddenly in control of an online digital distribution service. It could have become a great online service once it was owned by the music industry. Then all the other major labels banded together to shut it down and in so doing, they opened the door to iTunes. The music industry was seduced by Steve Jobs and by iTunes and fell over itself to get into bed with Apple. As a result those guys probably didn't do the best job in the world when it came to the music industry's deal with Apple, back in the day. There's a tendency when something new and bright and shiny comes along to be dazzled by it and to agree with everything that's happening in that new, shiny world.

You have to constantly re-examine your business model and make sure it's relevant to the modern world. Every creative business at the moment, from book publishers to print journalism, film and television, is running the traditional business model, same as they've been for 50 years, alongside a brand new business model. There's the steady decline of the old business model against the steady rise of the new business model. I look forward to the day the growth in the new business model exceeds the decline of the old business model and then we'll know we're out of this recession. The music business has been coping with the recession for quite a long time but there are some interesting developments; digital sales are booming. What's exciting is seeing the growth of online streaming services,

which is a brand new business model and looks likely to lead to a bright future. In Scandinavia it's enabled the music industry to return to quite strong growth in the last couple of years.

I think we've moved to a place where people aren't interested in owning content anymore. We've moved to a place where ownership of creative content is no longer important but access to that creative content is; you don't need to own 5,000 CDs. You just need a mobile phone that has access to every record that has ever been made. I don't buy anything like as much music as I used to but I probably listen to more music than I ever have.

As far as our company is concerned, what we're selling primarily is recorded copyrights. People are still paying for use of the copyrights – they're just consuming those copyrights in a different way. Our business model has changed in that we're no longer making money solely from the sale of those recorded copyrights, we're acknowledging that we're also building brands. We're responsible for creating successful artist-brands, and because we're so intrinsic to the creation of that brand we want to be earning revenue from all elements of that brand's business. We want to be earning from live, merchandising and brand partnerships. If it wasn't for the investment in both expertise and finance that the record companies are putting into the artist and the brand, the artist wouldn't be in this business, so we're looking for some financial acknowledgment of our input.

Brand is important and for some artists the brand is more important than the music. Gaga is arguably one of the biggest brands at the moment. Is the brand overpowering the music? I think the brand has always been there. Was the brand of Elvis Presley more important than the music he made? Absolutely, because he ended up making movies and his music was ultimately a means to promote the films. The relationship between brand and music has always existed.

Illegal file-sharing has been a big change to hit the industry. Some artists are OK about giving their music away for free because it helps to sell tickets and t-shirts. If they can fund that business model, that's great. That's not what we were set up to do (at Universal) and I don't think music should be free. I get frustrated that not enough is done with the current legislation to prosecute people who are stealing music.

In spite of the industry changes I still think it's a wonderful business to be involved in. I'm having as much fun as I ever had. When I was younger I would have sat up listening to music all night and playing CD after CD; now I sit in front of my computer and can quite easily be there at 3am just clicking on YouTube clip after YouTube clip and going through blogs. I'm still addicted to it! Long may it continue – I hope I'm still doing it when I'm 90!

NOW YOU KNOW…

- You know that your business operates in a market subject to consumer, technological and legal trends. You must be aware of the trends and how they affect your business. Pay attention to how your competitors are handling these trends. Their errors may become your opportunities.
- You are aware that trends can create disruption in established markets.

WHAT YOU'VE ACCOMPLISHED…

If you've completed the steps outlined in this chapter…

- You're now aware of trends that impact your business.
- You're aware of the trends your competitors are following.
- You know where and how to keep track of trends in the future.
- You've shown your resellers and marketing partners how your goods can help them take financial advantage of trends.

CHAPTER 5: THE CHANNEL

HOW DO WE REACH THEM?

HOW DO WE REACH THEM?

Most of us have heard the term 'sales channel' used to refer to finding stores that will carry your products and sell them to customers who happen to be passing by. But there are a wide variety of channels that can be used to find customers, introduce them to your product, deliver to them and support them after the sale.

You need to choose the channels that will suit your business and your brand to market, sell, support and deliver your work to your customers.

The channels you select to use will depend on your product, your industry, your brand and your target market. Be sure you understand your tightly-defined, fast-growing target market, and your competition, well before you invest a great deal of time and money in creating your channels. If the first channels you establish are the right ones, you should see an immediate increase in sales to new customers and from existing customers coming back to buy a second product. But if you start with a channel and don't have a clear idea of your customer, it's a bit like building a bridge without knowing where it might end. It's vital that you have a clear idea of where you're headed.

JARGON BUSTER

A channel is any business, social organisation or tool that connects you to your customers.

Traditional retail channels

Brick and mortar stores that sell directly to the public may buy products and services directly from a manufacturer or through a distributor. These resellers typically have 'buyers' who decide what to stock, how much to buy, and how payment will be made. To sell to buyers you need to deliver products and services that meet their needs and the needs of their customers.

PURE DISTRIBUTION CHANNELS

Distributors like Ingram Micro buy millions of products at the deepest discounts and sell them to resellers. They're in a position to give your business visibility because they can pair your product with other, related, more successful products. They also typically offer credit to their customers so you, as their supplier, don't have to worry about negotiating payment terms for each store they support. To sell to distributors you must deliver products and services that meet the needs of their buyers, reseller buyers and their customers.

If you have a premium product, a technical product or a product that requires training in order to ensure successful use, you might look at *restricted distribution*. Restricted distribution means, quite simply, that you restrict the distribution and the ways in which customers can access your product.

Restricted distribution is more common with a strong brand that wants to be perceived as high-end and exclusive. By restricting distribution, customers are aware that it's more difficult to purchase and not every retailer in the industry is permitted to sell it. These high-end brands are sensitive to not only where they are sold but also which brands and products they are sold next to, as the brand sitting alongside them is framing their product and customers may compare it and make associations in terms of both cost and quality.

VALUE ADDED DISTRIBUTION CHANNELS

Value added distributors sell your products and services on to resellers who sell them to customers.

For example, perhaps you sell a kind of counter tile for kitchens and bathrooms that is very expensive, very beautiful, and requires very special installation. You've trained many resellers who sell the tile and know how to install it, but now you want to sell a whole bunch more. In this case you might look for a value added distributor with a collection of high-end kitchen and bathroom resellers.

You can teach the value added distributor how to install your counter tiles, and they can then pass that knowledge on to their resellers. You have to give a percentage of each sale made to the resellers and the distributors, but hopefully you'll sell a lot more tiles as you'll have a lot more staff selling for you.

Before you sign an agreement with a value added distributor, make sure:

1. The deal you are considering is the most appropriate for your business.
2. That the company you are considering is capable of showing off your product or service and are motivated to sell it. Working on a commission is a good motivator.
3. That they are able to draw a large enough audience to sell to.
4. That you are prepared to pay both the distributor and reseller their percentage of the sale.

Your success relies on teaching those experts how and when to show your product.

VALUE ADDED RESELLER CHANNELS

These are resellers who take your product or service and add their own products and services to it in order to better meet the needs of the target market you both want to sell to.

Net-A-Porter (www.net-a-porter.com) have done a great job of value added distribution. They act as a stylist, they package clothing together, so they *add value* to the items. It's a compelling offer to a new designer, to know that their products will be styled and packaged up as outfits with pieces designed by others, to help the products sell.

If Net-A-Porter elect to sell your products, you will make a huge number of sales you would otherwise miss because they'll do such a good job of marketing your work for you to a group of customers who already trust them.

ONLINE SALES CHANNELS

These can be direct relationships between you and your customers through your company website, or they can be indirect relationships with your customers through third parties like Amazon, iTunes, eBay, Folksy, notonthehighstreet.com, Etsy and so on.

OFFLINE AFFILIATE CHANNELS

Independent businesses that actively promote products and services to customers they know, can act as your affiliates. Anybody can sign up to be an affiliate. Affiliates are essentially a bounty system. They drive audiences to you and you give them a bit of money each time. You determine how much you're willing to spend per customer and you pay the affiliate fee only when you get the customer. The one red light here is that if the affiliate is doing a great job, the main business will steal the affiliate's best ideas. So if your business is the affiliate, just make sure that where possible you don't give away your trade secrets. Affiliates are big business. There are companies whose whole business is to run affiliate programmes and track them.

AN AFFILIATE MARKETING TALE

A number of years ago, I was running my one day classes and I was talking about affiliate marketing schemes in particular, and how they can be a substitute for a channel of distribution. This was up in the North of England. A woman raised her hand and she said, 'Well, Doug, I'm a little puzzled because I just don't know what our affiliate marketing plan would be!'

I asked her what she sold and she told me that she and her husband ran a Bed & Breakfast. I asked her to tell me more about it. 'We're on the outskirts of a small town in Scotland and we're the second best B&B in town,' she said. I asked her how many B&Bs were in her town. She said two. I asked her about the brand position of her B&B. She told me her B&B was 'the one that's not as good as the other B&B in town'. I was intrigued. 'The other B&B,' she went on, 'is a lovely B&B up in the hills, it's got a Gothic feel about it, they have beautiful rooms and the view in the mornings is magnificent. Our B&B is part of the view downhill from the lovely B&B. The rooms are OK, the beds clean and the price per night is less.' I asked her how she found customers and she told me that sometimes,

when the nice B&B was full, they'd send customers they'd turned away to her B&B. I asked if that was the number one form of marketing and she said yes. Sometimes, she told me, customers didn't know about the lovely B&B and were disappointed in the morning when they realised there was a prettier place that they could have stayed in, just up the hill. I asked if there was anything else about her B&B that set it apart. She shook her head.

We talked about the decision-making process that leads a potential customer to drive through her town looking for accommodation. Usually customers are on their way from Edinburgh to Aberdeen, she told me, and if they start driving from Edinburgh late in the afternoon, it'll start to get dark. If they haven't made plans they'll need a place to sleep for the night. They'll

stop off for petrol and ask if there is somewhere they can stay for the night, or they'll stop at a tearoom and ask the same question.

Together we drew a map of the area which turned out to consist of a single road going from south to north and that was pretty much it apart from a few side roads. We added to the map the three petrol stations and four tearooms in this rather remote part of Scotland. I asked her if she knew the people who ran the petrol stations and the tearooms and she told me, like anyone from a small town, 'Of course!' So this is what I told her:

'I'd like you to print up a little card and write on it the details of your B&B with a little map of how people can find you. I want you to give these cards to the owners of the petrol stations and tearooms and on each card I want you to write the name of each place – so if it's Joe's petrol station that you're giving some cards to, write 'Joe's petrol station' on each card. Ask Joe if, next time somebody asks where they might stay for the night, he kindly give them this card. Tell him if he does, you'll give him a gift.'

She looked worried. 'I couldn't afford to give out gifts,' she said. 'We only charge £75 a night.'

'Ok,' I said, 'If someone comes and they give you a card courtesy of Joe, let's think about what you might give them. What do you do well? Can you cook?'

'No, my cooking is terrible,' she said.

'Can your husband do anything?' I asked.

'Oh!' she said, 'He's a fantastic baker, he makes great cupcakes.'

'Perfect!' I said. 'I want your husband to bake some cupcakes and give Joe a box of cupcakes as a thank you, when he recommends someone stay at your B&B.'

'This is the marketing plan?' she asked, bewildered.

'Yes,' I said. 'That's it.'

Six months later I got a postcard from her. 'Thank you Doug,' it read. 'Business is up through the roof! My husband has been making cupcakes and we've been handing them out; all the petrol stations and tearoom owners love us. We have to turn business away! We're considering raising our prices to £80 a night!'

That's affiliate marketing. You create a series of affiliates and they target customers for you. They become a channel of distribution.

I tell this story in particular because they seem like a business without an obvious affiliate marketing partner, when in fact there's a perfectly logical channel for them. You just have to ask yourself who can lead people to you and what can you do for them in return. If you're only making £75 a night then a cupcake is all you can realistically afford to offer as an incentive, but it's totally worth it.

ONLINE AFFILIATE CHANNELS

Often, online affiliates are people who run their own websites. They drive traffic to your online store and you give them a percentage of each sale. Commission Junction is an affiliate site worth exploring if online affiliates are the route your business should take (www.uk.cj.com).

AGENCIES

Unlike resellers, agencies represent you in the sale of your work but the profits go directly to you and then you pay the agency commission. A fashion showroom is basically an agency in fashion industry talk.

If you are a writer, actor, fine artist, musician or designer, a good agency can help you reach distant markets, new markets or markets that appear closed. Finding a good agency requires research and care. A bad agent is often far worse than no agent at all.

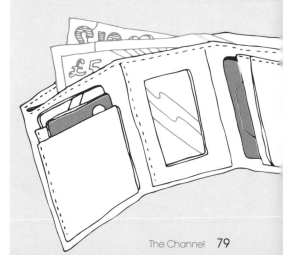

CONSIGNMENT CHANNELS

If you want to sell products to a retailer – and let's say it's a nice, small retailer – and you're trying to persuade them to pick up your beautiful, handmade goods, you need to prove they will sell. Unfortunately, it's not enough to just offer 'sale or return' to the retailer.

For those small retail stores, every single shelf has a clock on it and that clock is ticking. Every month the retailer pays rent for the space. If the stock you give them doesn't sell, you've cost the retailer in two different ways. Firstly you took their money in exchange for your stock, so they couldn't buy other things that would sell and make a profit. Secondly, they paid for a shelf for you, and your stuff just sat there. The core risk of being a retailer is in curating the right goods that will sell. Every shelf therefore has to earn its monthly shelf keep and pay its monthly rent contribution.

When you sell on consignment, you and the reseller split the risk. You put your goods on the reseller's shelf but you don't take any money up front. The retailer sells the goods and *only when the goods sell* will the retailer pay you. In a consignment relationship, the risk and cost to the retailer is reduced dramatically and you earn a higher profit on goods sold.

Once you've built a reputation and your stock is selling, you're absolutely right to approach the retailer and negotiate going back to sale or return, because you've proven your worth and they know that your stock sells.

Note that you can set up consignment deals with anyone who wants to show your work to people in return for a percentage of the revenue if it sells.

JARGON BUSTER

Sale or return is an agreement with the retailer that says they can return any goods to you that aren't sold and you will reimburse them.

JARGON BUSTER

Consignment is when you give a product to a reseller for free and when they sell it they give you the lion's share of the revenue.

MULTI-LEVEL MARKETING CHANNELS

Avon cosmetics, Amway cleaning products and Tupperware food containers made this model famous. Multi-level marketing is a form of affiliate marketing that allows people who love a product to sell it to their friends, families and business associates. Some of those people may love the product so much they decide to become resellers as well. Each person then becomes part of a pyramid of people distributing the product.

This is a legal activity if the overall sales are made to end customers. It is illegal if the only customers ever in the transaction are people who buy your products hoping to sell them to others but never manage to do so. That is called a pyramid scheme.

Multi-level marketing can be an effective way to sell certain products.

FAIRS, TRADE SHOWS AND OPEN MARKET CHANNELS

The entrepreneurs who run fairs, trade shows and open markets invite dozens, hundreds or sometimes even thousands of potential customers to buy products and services from providers who pay to have a booth or a stall at a given event. This is a great method for reaching a large audience with a very specific interest.

AWARENESS CHANNELS

These channels introduce potential customers to products and services without any push to buy them. Car showrooms, perfume ads in magazines, flagship stores on streets where retail space is at a premium, are examples of awareness channels at work. You can create your own awareness channels by running events through Meetup.com, Eventbrite.com and by working with clubs or organisations that reach your customers every day.

Sometimes a channel can be a subtle thing. Why does Levi's have a store on Regent Street in central London? Is it really the best place for them to be commercially? I doubt it. Regent Street is one of the three of four most important retail streets in the world and one of the most expensive to rent. Retail space in the UK generally is some of the costliest in the world and as my friend Theo Paphitis has said, the only people who make money in retail are the landlords. The prestige of Regent Street and the ability of Levi's to create a shop that displays all their goods in their own environment makes it worth the huge overheads. This is an example of retail being used as an awareness channel for the Levi's brand.

VISIBILITY

A *visibility partner* is a company that buys your product or service at just above cost, for resale to their customers as part of a promotion. When you work with a visibility partner, ensure your contract specifies that your company name and product name remain part of the product and the company's marketing campaign. You benefit because hundreds, thousands or millions of people learn about your product and some percentage of those people actually get to try it. Your partner benefits because they get to provide a great product or service to their customers at a substantial discount and make a profit in the process. In effect your company receives a great advertising campaign without paying for it in cash. Visibility partners are an awareness channel. Startups benefit greatly when they work with visibility partners so you should actively look for those relationships in the months and years to come.

EVALUATION CHANNELS

Evaluation channels allow customers to try products before they buy them. Marketing companies that send out free trials or coupons to potential customers for their clients who are advertisers, are serving as evaluation channels. *Which?* magazine, the consumer advocacy, non-profit evaluator of white goods, electrical goods and other household items, is an evaluation channel. Restaurant reviewers are evaluators; bloggers have become the new wave of evaluators. Don't be scared of the blogger community; neither ingratiate yourself with them, nor offend them. Involve them, talk to them, let them try out your product or service. Good products will find a market with enough exposure.

TECHNICAL SUPPORT CHANNELS

Technical support channels increase customer satisfaction, reduce product return rates, and help encourage future sales. Sometimes a technical support channel is just a phone number on the back of a shipping box that lets people talk to someone at your office who can help them solve a problem with a product. Sometimes a technical support channel is a whole office full of people who do nothing but help customers install, use, and maintain products they've purchased.

A great technical support channel is an excellent way to ensure that a customer who makes a purchase from you gets the help they need when they need it, ensuring their satisfaction with both the product and the service, and making them repeat customers.

If you don't want to or are unable to provide technical support, there are many call centres you can hire to provide it for you.

DELIVERY CHANNELS

Delivery channels get products to customers. They ensure objects arrive in the right packaging, provide shipping information to customers and help people track missing shipments. Courier companies are delivery channels, as is the Royal Mail.

There are also pick, pack, and ship companies who will warehouse and ship your products to customers for a fixed price per order. These companies are an excellent resource for enterprises who need to be able to ship a lot of products to a lot of people without having to hire a whole staff to do it. You might be surprised to know that Amazon Fulfilment will pick, pack and ship your products worldwide.

GET YOUR HANDS DIRTY

Try this: Take a look at the channels your competitors are using to reach customers and determine which appear to work best and why.

Based on what you've learned from studying competitors and reading this chapter, think about which channels might work best to sell your products and explore options for creating them. Decide which sales channels will work best in the short and long term.

Determine which channels you will use to create awareness of your products within your target market and decide what channels you want to use to deliver and support your products and services going forward.

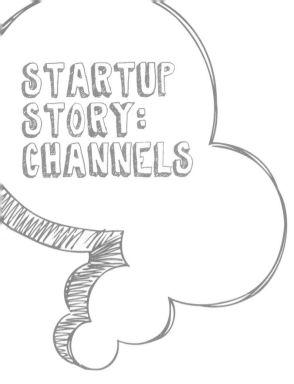

STARTUP STORY: CHANNELS

ASHLEY LONG

FINANCE DIRECTOR,
PAUL SMITH LTD

www.paulsmith.co.uk

Paul Smith has been in business for over 40 years and today there are 14 different collections wholesaled to 70 countries, with shops around the world including London, Milan, Paris, New York and Tokyo. Designed in Nottingham and London, the Paul Smith collections are primarily produced in Europe while the fabrics used are mainly of Italian and British origin. Paul remains both designer and chairman and is continually involved in every aspect of the business.

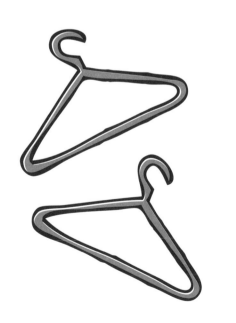

The first clothes that Paul ever made were white shirts because the only fabric you could buy in a few metres was white poplin. He didn't have the sales to buy 150 metres of a nice stripe or gingham so he bought white poplin and put red buttons on it. He opened his first shop in Nottingham in the early 1970s and within a matter of months he was taking his first wholesale order for Bergdorf Goodman in New York. Very early on it was clear that what was needed was scale.

Paul wouldn't know what a 'channel' was; he's very anti-jargon. His view of business, fashion and the world is quite simple really; it's all about balance. I've worked for Paul for 21 years and throughout that time we've always talked about the tripod. One leg of the tripod is retail – or our own retail. You need your own shops so you can show the world the whole of what you do, with maximum control. It's profitable if you get it right, costly if you get it wrong but it allows you to turn things into cash quickly. You don't have to wait to be paid. There are lots of things you can do with retail.

When Paul took the first shop on Floral Street in Covent Garden in 1979, there was nothing there, it was an abandoned area. Now it's in the heart of a thriving tourist area. There's no magic formula. As canny as you can be about the next location to go for in retail, you need a bit of good fortune too. We *hate* closing shops; we try and get it as right as we can. We want interesting buildings, interesting neighbours and hopefully some footfall!

The second leg of the tripod is wholesale. That's been our dominant channel and it still is; it's two-thirds of our business. I think a lot of that is our place in history. Paul Smith really expanded in the nineties and the early 2000s on the back of an explosion of menswear boutiques and department stores. We've ridden that wave, to a degree. Would we do that now? I don't think the opportunity is the same now. Wholesale is a much harder place. Small boutiques are very fickle; they want the 'newest', they want exclusivity, which for a brand like ours is very difficult. Department stores are also demanding and it's becoming more costly. The wholesale model has developed into franchising more than traditional wholesale; it's a neat hybrid. You end up with a shop, albeit you don't own the shop but you control what it looks like design wise, and you can add your personality.

When we open a Paul Smith shop in another country, we usually already have a wholesale business there as we sell in 70 countries. So we've usually got an inkling that our own retail will work. If we're doing well at wholesale, we know we ought to be able to do well at our own retail. It's less true if you're opening in somewhere like Saudi Arabia or Korea or the Philippines. In those countries you're

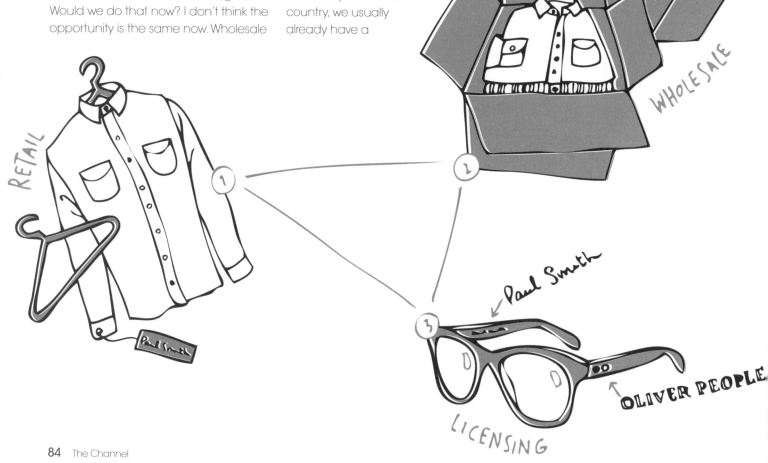

RETAIL

WHOLESALE

← Paul Smith

↑ OLIVER PEOPLE

LICENSING

more reliant on finding a good partner who has a solid proposition, someone with a track record and something they can hang their hat on, rather than pots of money. Deal with like-minded people, would be my advice; someone who you think you can trust. If you don't like someone then it's probably best not to do business with them! We've only had one partnership that went sour and that was 20 years ago in the USA; that was a clash of cultures. Other than that we've been quite lucky.

The third leg of our tripod has always been licensing. Licensing for us started with our inability to manage a wholesale business in Japan. We couldn't react to their delivery schedule and we couldn't accommodate another load of sizing, we just didn't have the resource. So license was a sensible thing to do. It came out of necessity rather than vision. We were lucky that we had a good partnership with an enormous company in Japan that, although they didn't really know about licensing either, had lots of resources. They've always just done what we've asked them to do. Paul first went to Japan in 1982 and he's been there every six months since, which is unheard of for a designer. We have an office there now. In Japan, your first proper job equals a Paul Smith suit, that's a given.

Subsequent to that, licensing has been about specialist products – the stuff that we can't do, like watches. We tried to make watches but realised it was too complex. In those instances it's far better to have a nice licence partner who really understands watches. It's the same with luggage and spectacles. The Paul Smith specs that are sold through David Clulow for example, are from a licensee with a very small, specialist company called Oliver Peoples in L.A. The challenge for Oliver Peoples – and now for us – is that they've been successful and they've been bought, first by Oakley and then by Luxottica. That could be great, or it could change the dynamic. We just have to wait and see.

Over the years we've found that none of those three tripod legs – retail, wholesale and licensing – are growing at the same time but likewise they've never all gone down at the same time – so that's the balance! Nowadays you'd probably add a fourth leg to the tripod, which is online. We started our website in 2004. In the fashion industry, brands were slow to come online and department stores even slower. In 2004 people already knew Paul's name – they knew the 'brand', although Paul would hate that term! We didn't have trouble finding visitors to the site but we've focused on converting visitors to shoppers over the last couple of years and that's become a science in itself. You're not only selling to your fan base but trying to grow more visitors each month and find ways to convince visitors to spend their money. Online marketing has become the monster that you have to keep feeding. We have lots of young people who work for us and who live and breathe that digital world and we have to let them run riot a little bit. There is an upside though, which is that you can see the results quite clearly, through analytics. It's comforting from a financial perspective to be able to see what works.

We're re-launching our website soon as the competition is so great, we can't just stay still. Retailers are very critically judged on their websites and we know we have a real asset in Paul himself – he's an absolute human dynamo – so little film clips of him talking or explaining things will be something real and unique. People naturally want to find things that are new and interesting. They'll stay on the website through clever communication, humour and interest but it's hard to keep your sense of humour online without looking slapstick!

We make sure that Paul Smith products are sold consistently across all channels because we have contractual control. We sign off every shop, we design it ourselves. We also have staff who go around the world supporting but also policing our brand. We also control all our own press. We have press officers in London, Paris, Milan, New York and Tokyo. All our franchise partners and licensees get their Paul Smith press from us. That does sound very controlling but it's also a service, it does something for them as well.

We've just signed a franchise agreement with China; the first franchise store has just opened with another 25 planned over the next five years. That's not a huge number by Burberry standards but we want to grow sustainably. We'd like to take a breather and take our foot off the gas, but the reality is that businesses go either up or down, they don't go straight along in level flight. We're not overly aggressive on growth plans; we'd rather have a nice, stable, sustainable business that people thought was great. Sometimes even we're surprised. We've got 25 shops in Korea, for example, which is incredible. We're successful and it's nothing to be embarrassed about but it really isn't the sole aim of the business. We want something that's got longevity, which is why Paul has never sold. Our turnover is £200m so we look at Burberry on £1.8bn and think, 'See, we can grow loads!'

Paul's name on the business does hold us back a little as Paul will tell you he's a person, not a brand. He doesn't want to see his name in some horrible shop somewhere; he does worry about what he should put his name on. We had our misgivings about luggage for example; it's the most boring part of the department store! Could we make the luggage section a bit more rock and roll? It's a challenge.

Sometimes we think of the products that we want to collaborate on and sometimes we're approached to see if we want to lend our designs to a product. We rely on gut instinct. Creating a line in Paul Smith tea towels might be very profitable for us but it's not where we want to go. There always has to be a point. Sometimes the point is just fun, like the Evian bottles: 12 bottles with 12

different coloured lids. Paul would say he wouldn't want to do anything that could result in a nasty letter. That's where he would draw the line.

We've got a good feeling for what sells and what people like but we don't do hardcore research. The digital age has given us more of an idea of who actually buys our product. Often it gives us more of a shock than anything else. We're lucky that we have a very wide following and there seems to be a youthful following as well. When you're young you don't tend to have as much money so that's why we have a jeans collection to attract the younger market on the basis of both style as well as price.

We know we have a scattergun approach to product and customers which is a great asset but also a great hurdle because you have to make an awful lot of things, explain an awful lot of things. Your greatest asset can be your greatest weakness. It comes back to balance, all the time.

"Some Thoughts"

1. Start something new
2. Take pleasure seriously
3. Work is not about shorter hours or longer hours, it's about EVERY hour
4. You can't do it, without doing it
5. Make room to break the rules
6. Stop making sense, logic is predictable, think differently
7. Make NEW mistakes, better mistakes, mistakes that make a difference
8. Every burden is a gift

Paul Smith

NOW YOU KNOW...

- You know that some channels, like retail sales channels, come with costs you must be aware of and consider when discovering your sale price.
- You know about all the different routes to market and awareness channels and which routes are most appropriate for your business.
- You recognise that visibility partners who promote your products and brand to their customers in return for your very best pricing may drive a lot of traffic to your website where people can buy directly from you in the future. This is one of the best ways to dramatically increase sales quickly at a very low cost.
- You see how technical support and delivery channels can be critical to subsequent sales to the same customers and referral to new customers.

WHAT YOU'VE ACCOMPLISHED...

If you've completed the steps outlined in this chapter...

- You have decided which channels you should begin to use immediately in order to jump-start your sales.
- You've started looking for a visibility partner because you know they are key to creating a strong startup quickly. Most often this will mean you should look for a company who sells to your target market already. Approach them with an offer to provide your product for 10% to 20% over your cost in return for their mention of your brand in all promotion. You want to create a win-win solution in return for them promoting you.
- You're exploring cost-effective delivery, support and resale relationships to help ease your load and cost and improve your visibility and customer experience.

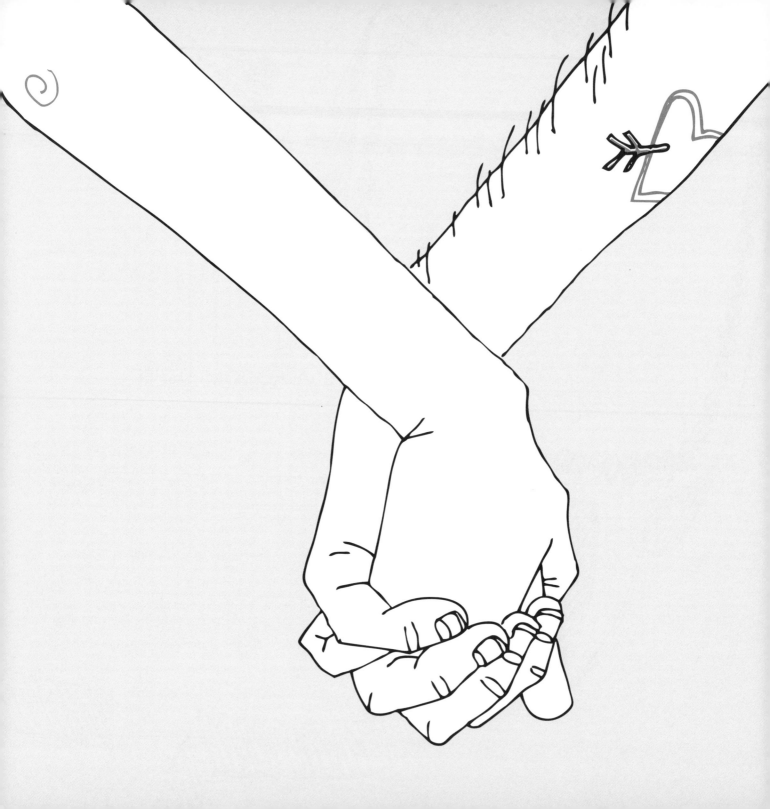

CHAPTER 6: THE RELATIONSHIP

WHAT FINANCIAL RELATIONSHIP DO YOU WANT WITH YOUR CUSTOMER?

WHAT FINANCIAL RELATIONSHIP DO YOU WANT WITH YOUR CUSTOMER?

How people pay for what you sell can make a tremendous difference to the profitability of your company. Careful consideration of what your company sells, under what terms and to whom, can turn a good business idea into a hugely successful enterprise.

Every business creates one or more financial relationships with its customers. Choosing the right form for that relationship is paramount to making sure that the business thrives. In some cases, slightly modifying your product to suit a different customer type can ramp up your business success.

For example, at School for Creative Startups we sell our entrepreneurs' training and support in a variety of ways. We occasionally run short courses and boot camps that people pay full price to attend. We also run short courses, boot camps, six-month and twelve-month courses which are subsidised by government, commercial, educational and philanthropic organisations and for which people pay only a nominal fee to attend. We sell our content in videos, books and ebooks. We create custom content based on our curricula, for others to sell.

If you consider that shortlist you'll realise we are repackaging our content in a variety of forms to meet the needs of a variety of customers. In some cases we accept a fixed price for a course, in other cases we accept a subscription payment. Sometimes we publish content for a fixed fee and other times we license it for a royalty.

Some of the most profitable businesses in existence today were created by taking something people purchased regularly and then changing the way in which they paid for it. Netflix and LoveFilm, as we discussed earlier, all but replaced Blockbuster Video, simply by finding a way to change the financial relationship under which their customers rented movies.

An introduction to revenue models

A revenue model lays out how your product or service will be packaged, who it will be sold to, and how you will be paid. Pricing models and revenue models work hand in hand to help you figure out how to sell your work in the most profitable way and at the most profitable price.

An author can sell his or her work as a series of stories for a magazine, as a book, or as a series of spoken-word theatrical events. Those are three different revenue models and each targets a different kind of customer. A magazine editor would pay the author for the series of stories; a publisher would pay the author for the book; and a theatre company might pay the playwright by sharing a percentage of the box office revenue each time the play is performed. This is called a 'rev share' agreement. Each of those revenue models will have its own pricing model. A magazine editor will most likely pay a fixed fee for the right to use a story, whereas a publisher would usually pay the author a royalty on each book they sell. The theatre-goers would pay a fixed price to see a play and thus the theatre company would pay the author a fixed price to be able to perform the play. There are a huge number of revenue models you can use as you build your business. Choosing the right one could generate a healthy profit, pretty fast.

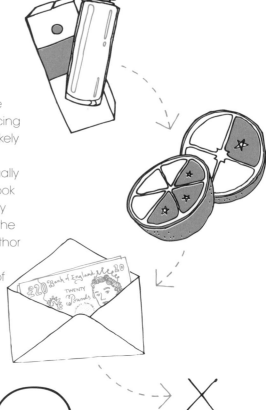

JARGON BUSTER!

A *revenue model* is a plan for how you will package your product or service for sale, who you will sell it to, how you will be paid, and how often you will be paid.

TYPES OF REVENUE MODELS:
Retail sales
Consulting
Fixed fee for service
Use fees, lending, renting, leasing
Subscription
Shared Ownership
Licensing
Brokerage/Agent
Franchise fees
Advertising

IMPACT ON YOU AND YOUR CUSTOMERS

Let's say you buy a book from a bookshop and you read the book. You could then sell the book to a second hand bookshop. You have a right to sell the book because you own the book. When the bookshop charged you, they charged you a given amount for outright ownership of that individual book. But what happens if you buy the electronic version of the book? What do you own? In this instance, you can't sell the book. It's impractical and it's illegal. You didn't buy the right to sell it. You didn't even buy the right to keep it. Essentially, you bought a long-term lease on the ebook. If you bought it from, say, Amazon, and for any reason there's a problem with the book they could actually take it back. Poof! It's gone from your Kindle.

You need to decide in the modern world, what exactly are you selling and what rights are you handing over to other people when they pay you?

RETAIL SALES REVENUE MODEL

Customers purchase your product from you or one of your resellers by paying for it once. Done. This one's easy.

FIXED FEE FOR SERVICE REVENUE MODEL

Often people purchase a specific service and don't require that you or your operatives spend a fixed period of time doing it. They make more when they work faster. Wedding dressmakers often offer brides-to-be a bespoke gown and two fittings, for a fixed price.

CONSULTING REVENUE MODEL

Customers purchase your services on an hourly, daily, weekly or monthly basis. Copywriters often work under these terms.

USE FEES, LENDING, RENTING AND LEASING REVENUE MODELS

Hotel rooms, theme parks and couriers are all priced based on use. How much time a customer spends using a location, facilities or resources determines how much they pay. Some businesses choose to lend their work rather than sell it.

SUBSCRIPTION REVENUE MODEL

Subscription fees have become really popular again. In the US and increasingly in the UK, you can subscribe to consumables like coffee, pet food, wine – pretty much anything you buy repeatedly. *The Economist* magazine allows people to pay a fixed fee over a given period of time for access to the content they want.

SHARED OWNERSHIP REVENUE MODEL

Under this business model, an enterprise creates an infrastructure that allows people to share ownership of an item or location. Timeshare holidays and, as we discussed earlier in the book, NetJets and Zipcar are all based on this business model. Their customers share use of a given item or location for a specified period of time.

LICENSING REVENUE MODEL

Under this business model, people pay for the use of carefully identified intellectual property for a set period of time. It can be a film, an audio track, an image or a character. Unlike the sale of intellectual property, which also includes the exchange of the property for a given price, a licence deal states explicitly the start and end of the agreement and outlines the acceptable use for the intellectual property. Many licensing agreements 'rubber band', which means if the purchaser doesn't hit a given performance target, or uses intellectual property in an unauthorised way, the rights revert back to the intellectual property owner straight away. Filmmakers and artists, authors, actors and designers license their property to others. Sometimes businesses choose to license well-known intellectual property to increase the value of the products and services they make.

BROKERAGE REVENUE MODEL

Talent agencies and art galleries are examples of brokerage firms. They represent a person, or the work of a person, to potential customers. Often, in the case of art galleries, they get access to the artwork that they showcase in the gallery for free and return a percentage of any purchase to the artist. Credit cards can be seen as a form of brokerage as well. They allow customers to purchase products they could not otherwise afford and charge both the customer a fee and the reseller a fee for serving as a financing middleman.

FRANCHISE FEE MODEL

This is about selling the rights for someone else to invest and grow and manage a version of your business. Usually the way the franchise model works, you sell the methodology but then you demand that people buy various ingredients and elements required by that methodology from you. The reason people adopt franchise models is usually because their business needs to expand and they can't pay for the expansion themselves.

Say you own a hugely successful healthy burger cafe and want to raise the money to open 1,000 more cafes. It's unlikely you'd get the capital from your bank so instead you cut a deal. With the franchise model, the person who realises a franchise pays for the lease on the building and finds the capital for their cafe. This person – the franchisee – gets to share the management of the whole operation because they've invested capital in it. They create the cafe from their own money and they buy from your healthy burger company the name, the brand, the method, the look and the rules. The benefit to the franchisee (the person who is running the franchise cafe on your company's behalf) is that your healthy burger company has created the drive and desire for the healthy burgers. Franchising is a complicated model and it can be very hard to get right. You can grow faster through this type of cookie-cutter franchise business as long as the core model works and assuming you can create the overarching demand. Bear in mind, though, that you do have less control in this scenario.

If you're going global, there are some countries where a franchise model might be the only option to access a new market. In Saudi Arabia and UAE, for example, a foreign corporation can't own more than 50% of a company, so a franchise might be the only way to reach that market. Franchises usually come into play when there is large physical infrastructure, like a shop, a building, or some land.

ADVERTISING

The basic principle of advertising is selling others the opportunity to distribute their message on your space. You gather up an audience and then sell access to that audience to those who wish to reach your specific target market. You're not selling a product, you're selling the right of access to that group of people that you have proprietary access to.

Now that you've reviewed a wide variety of revenue models and pricing models you should have some thoughts about how your business might best make a profit. To figure out which options are going to work, you'll need to do one or more financial forecasts. This is where you calculate how much you're going to earn and how much you're going to spend, to see if you can make a profit and grow it over time.

GET YOUR HANDS DIRTY
Try this:

ONE

Study all the revenue models your competitors have created to serve your fastgrowing, easily-accessible market.

TWO

Write down which are new or unique and figure out why this new business model might be better for customers and for the businesses that offer them.

THREE

Analyse how much each revenue model is likely to earn based on what you know about your customers. Pay attention to those that seem like they'd be significantly more profitable because they would significantly increase sales or reduce costs.

FOUR

Decide which revenue models you want to offer your customers initially and consider which options you want to offer them over time. For example, you may decide that you want to specialise in selling subscriptions to clothing for children so they get a new box of clothes every month. You might then decide this is something a grandparent, aunt or uncle is likely to buy for a child, and you would modify your marketing plans to accommodate what you have determined to be the most profitable revenue model.

STARTUP STORY: THE RELATIONSHIP

TONY ELLIOTT
FOUNDER AND CHAIRMAN, *TIME OUT*
www.timeout.com

Tony Elliott is the founder and chairman of Time Out, which began life as a fortnightly A5 folded poster *Time Out* to showcase the best of the alternative culture developing in London in the late 1960s. As Time Out expanded, Tony licensed the Time Out brand, which can now be found in 28 countries, 25 of which are managed by licensees. In 2010, Elliott sold 50% of the business to Oakley Capital. And in September 2012, *Time Out London* became a free magazine, distributing over 300,000 free copies each week.

In the summer of 1968 Time Out was born. I was interested in all the new cultural activity that was going on. I don't know what you'd call it now – independent culture probably. Back then it was called alternative or underground. Fringe theatre had just arrived. Finding all the information in one place was impossible and the established media – from the weekly music papers to the *Evening Standard* and the *Observer* – didn't really cover the new wave, really interesting stuff. There was a healthy underground press, with titles like *International Times (IT)*, *Oz*, *Black Dwarf* and other fringe publications which were a good source of information - but they didn't really have any proper listings.

I was interested in information and organising it in a fresh, clear essential way. When we started there was this magazine called *What's On* but it was a bit dull. Their commercial structure was totally based on the advertisers, their listings were compiled mainly of those who would advertise, so it was skewed. It's always an error to start the business with an advertiser's or sponsor's needs, and not the needs of the audience as the priority.

What I did, certainly in the beginning, was to say, 'There's all this activity going on, what's the best that's available?' We picked out the best of the conventional, established culture, stuff like the National Theatre, the Royal Shakespeare Company, the Royal Court, certain good West End films, important music events, etc, and married that with the best of what was called the contemporary counter culture, and we created a brand new type of publication.

It had a brilliant response from most people often saying 'why hasn't anyone done this before?'. In a sense that's one reason why it worked. It was genuinely filling a hole that maybe a lot of people didn't realise was there. We kind of knew from the first issue of *Time Out* that it was working. We started small, we were just in London, and the number of copies we sold in the beginning was about 5,000.

It's been more difficult since the Internet came along and there's been an explosion of print publications, like all the free weekend newspaper supplements. Whereas we had a distinct patch that we occupied in the early days, nowadays it's a lot more crowded. However, I still think we're unique. I think Time Out has this drive to provide information that people want. I always ask, 'Is it useful?'. We often hear our regular readers refer to *Time Out* as 'my Bible' which is heartening, as we know we're needed.

Over the years a large number of people have remained loyal readers but there have always been continuous waves of new readers. We've always had a healthy number of students with often around 8–12% of the readership at any time. We became a free magazine on 25 September 2012 and the readership data shows that the number of young readers has radically increased, which is probably because they couldn't afford it when it was a paid magazine.

There's been remarkable consistency in our readership over 44 years with healthy numbers of people in the 17–35 age range. The gender split has varied; today it's 60% women but it's often been 50/50. Those stats don't inform the content though. We feel that we've got a pretty normal demographic so what we write is less driven by what we know about our readership and who they are and more about the Time Out view of the world.

We don't differentiate between expensive and cheap activities, we just ask, 'Is it any good?' All our editorial staff are specialists in particular areas and on top of what's new. The readers will often tell us what they want; they're very opinionated and that's good. But we still maintain our own opinion.

There has never been any relationship between our advertisers and content, no matter how big the advertisers are or how much money they stump up. Our independence is a marker of our integrity. No one can buy their way into our rankings. I've always been incredibly determined that we should be independent.

The only audience with any leverage is our readers'; if they didn't think we were doing a good job, they would tell us and that would be it. Since *Time Out London* became a free magazine, the users are our readers, and the customers who pay for it to be published are our advertisers. But the needs of the users (readers) are always our priority.

We've always had to get a certain level of advertising to produce the magazine. Now that we're free, really simply, the ad rate has doubled. Our circulation has gone from 55,000 to 300,000 and the advertisers pay at least double the old rate, even though they're now advertising to six times the audience. There's usually an inbuilt discount around free publications because it's not the exactly the same kind of audience as when people pay for the content.

The majority of advertisers were encouraging in our switch from paid to free because they could see the benefit in getting access to a bigger and good quality audience. Advertisers who had semi-stopped advertising with us, because our reach wasn't big enough for them, have come back to

us. I'm a little worried about whether some of our smaller advertisers can afford to advertise with us regularly now that the rate has doubled. I think we'll be OK as long as they perceive that the quality of the audience is as good as it was before. And it's a much bigger audience now with a million people consuming Time Out every week.

The feedback so far on our content through the free magazine has been really encouraging. The content has changed – we don't publish the same in-depth information that formed the basis for me starting the business in 1968 but that's because it's now all available online.

It was hard work developing our online audience in 1994/5, but we're moving now from print to exclusively online in some new cities. We've just done Time Out Los Angeles and that's online only, as is Time Out Paris. It's no different for our editors and wiriters in collating their hit-list of where to go and what to do, but we are moving towards adding user-generated commentary and more interactive content. We'll still be monitoring whether the comments are viable and fit properly.

We have nearly 6 million unique monthly visitors to the London website, which is great. I think people come to any Time Out website to get a simple answer to a simple question and that's what I try to drill into my team as the foundation that Time Out online anywhere is based upon.

We've done research and focus groups with our readers over the years and some feedback that we kept hearing was that they felt overwhelmed by the sheer amount of things there were to do in *Time Out*. So by simplifying the printed version we've answered that need. The latest weekly edition keeps you connected without overwhelming you. It's now the printed weekly *Time Out* guide to the huge guide which is on timeout.com.

People need to feel as though they belong; to feel part of a community having shared experiences and since the beginning I think we've answered that emotional need. We don't shy away from talking about a 'secret' this or 'pop-up' that at the risk of inundating those new places with visitors and making them less secret! If it's good, we'll give it a mention.

With our expansion, we always say that a city is potentially viable for Time Out in print or online because there's a nightclub, great bars, and dynamic restaurant scene emerging alongside a strong cultural and artistic base. There are certain places that we really want to be; in Seoul, South Korea for example, but we haven't found the right person to manage it. Mexico City was a market we were looking into for ages and have now entered with a local licencee, but we never just invade a place and set up a magazine or website. Sometimes people pitch to us and tell us they want to run Time Out in their city. Tel Aviv for example, is a small territory economically, but a great magazine.

Anyone who's doing Time Out in a foreign place produces their local,

customised version that taps into the local psyche. Underpinning it all is our directive that it be independent, comprehensive, follows the core template and ensuring the quality and character is consistent. We are a lot more demanding now about specifying there has to be a good website. There's an implicit expectation of what they're going to do in terms of quality.

In lots of cases it's self-selecting because the people that approach us to get a licence to produce Time Out

in their country, have seen Time Out in other countries and really 'get it'. They want to be 'Time Out' in their territory. Nowadays with the Time Out business, the organisation, anything it produces has the right look, feel, DNA etc. We've had a lot of very good people over the last four decades who have worked on it.

I don't think anybody anywhere in the world does information like Time Out does.

NOW YOU KNOW...

- You understand that you can create a wide variety of financial relationships with your customers and that choosing a relationship that offers customers advantages, could make your company both profitable and competitive.
- You see how you can package, price and sell your work in a variety of ways, all at the same time.
- You're paying attention to how your competitors structure their financial relationships with customers, because they may come up with a new way for people to pay for things that undercuts your offering dramatically.

WHAT YOU'VE ACCOMPLISHED...

If you've completed the steps outlined in this chapter...

- You've checked out your competition to see what they do well when it comes to creating a financial relationship with your target market.
- You've chosen the financial relationships that you want to create with customers first and you're looking ahead at which relationships you might want to grow on with these customers, or other customers, as your company grows.

CHAPTER 7:
THE PRICING MODEL

WHAT IS IT WORTH TO THEM?

WHAT IS IT WORTH TO THEM?

In this chapter you'll learn how to set prices for your work. Discovering the right price for your product or service requires careful thinking, a little research and some analysis, but it's one of the most important decisions you'll make as you start your business. Take my advice: correcting a poorly set price after you've set it is very difficult.

When you set the price for a product or a service, it creates an 'anchor' in the minds of your customers. They'll make an association between the product/service and the price. If you launch a product and then make a radical price change, either up or down, potential customers will distrust the value of what you sell and the integrity of your enterprise. In many cases the only way to fix a poorly set price is to come out with a new version of your product/service with a new name and entirely new marketing materials. You often have to 'reboot' a product completely, to justify a new price.

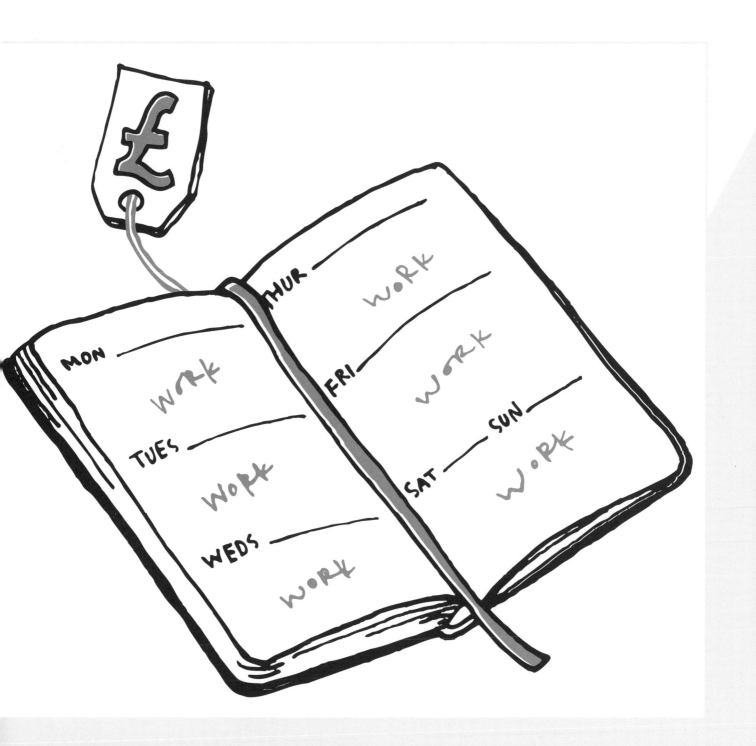

Price and cost

There are two steps to setting your price. Firstly, work out the price your market is willing to pay for what you want to sell. Secondly, make sure that your running costs will not run away with your profit! In other words, can you can sell your product or service to customers, cover all of your costs and still make a profit?

A common mistake made by the aspiring entrepreneur is thinking that their running costs alone should set the price that customers pay. The truth is that your customers don't care what your costs are. When they want to buy something, they'll buy the product that best meets their needs from the vendor with the right price. Unfortunately, your costs don't factor in the price they choose to pay.

The other common pitfall for the new entrepreneur is overlooking how much their time costs their business. I had one student at School for Creative Startups who was adamant that her online publication had zero costs. She hadn't considered the cost and value of her time. Every month that she chose to work for herself and not to work for someone else, she was giving up an income that she could have earned. Her online publication could never be successful until it paid her more than the potential revenue from employment that she was missing out on. Understanding the precious value of her time helped her to think about new ways – beyond accepting ads in her publications – to generate revenue from her site.

If you calculate your business costs on the basis that you'll always be working for free, then you'll create a business that can never support you. Your costs don't set your price but they do play a part in the kind of business that you can afford to run. Since you're just starting out, you can make a choice to produce products and services that will sell at a high enough price to pay you well. Simply put, if you find making tin whistles doesn't pay much, maybe have a rethink and pick something to sell that pays a little better. Now is the time to seriously consider this; it's a long way back when you've trundled on with your business, only to find your product doesn't make a penny profit and barely covers your costs.

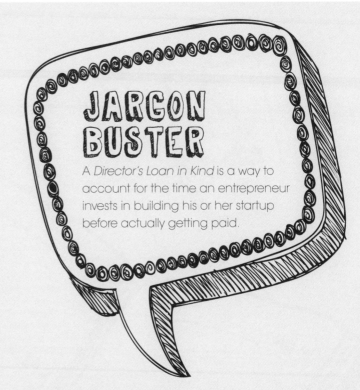

JARGON BUSTER

A *Director's Loan in Kind* is a way to account for the time an entrepreneur invests in building his or her startup before actually getting paid.

The way I factor a founder's salary into startup costs is that I set myself a realistic salary, which is the market value of the position that I'm filling. If that's £40K a year, I'll charge my business as though the £40K was being spent. On the balance sheet I record that the business owes me a year's salary. This is called a *director's loan in kind*. In effect, you are loaning the business your time during the startup period.

Placing a cash value on your time and noting it in your cash flow documents and financial forecasts makes it a lot easier to create a business that can sustain you. Having the salary figure sitting squarely in your financial calculations forces you to look for opportunities and to take business deals that will actually pay you a living wage. Your pricing and cost calculations have to cover the very real cost of running your business so you need to make decisions that will generate a truly profitable startup.

SETTING YOUR PRICE

I have counselled and supported thousands of entrepreneurs over the years and something that never ceases to amaze me is how many of them initially enter the market with the intent of competing on price alone.

I've an extensive background in sales and marketing and, since I've managed more than my fair share of sales teams, I understand the need to maximize the number of high-value sales you can get. Those sales are the ones you should spend all your time trying to achieve. Setting your startup to be a 'low price leader' is like intentionally choosing to sell to the people who will pay you the least amount of money. This is a terrible mistake 99.5% of the time. In fact, startups should almost universally target the high end of a fast-growing, tightly defined, target market. Those customers will pay you a premium and the profits you earn will help you reach more customers quickly. That'll help your business grow stronger and more profitable.

I believe creative startups like you make the mistake of competing on price because you are desperate to do what you love for a living and you don't recognise the value of your work. Given that you have no training in how prices are set, why people buy what they buy, or how to find people who will pay them top dollar for what they do, it's hardly surprising that you think you should take the hit. In reading this book you should discover, happily, that you can get paid very well for doing what you love and that you never have to sell your time or your work for bottom dollar prices.

A startup should only become a low price leader if its founders have discovered a new way to dramatically reduce the costs of delivering a product or service to a large target market. In this instance a lower price is possible because the real business costs are lower. The founders should be able to comfortably pay themselves a living wage because they've scratched out some of the additional costs to the business.

In the US, you can watch films and television shows through Hulu (www.hulu.com) because they've negotiated online-only distribution with several hundred content providers. Hulu charges customers a small fee for access to all their content and that price is substantially lower than the cost of subscribing to a cable television service, because Hulu is ad supported. Hulu's business model is entirely new and thus they can charge much less than cable television channels and rental outlets offering the same content. As a high-tech startup, Hulu found a way to be a low price leader, but this is generally the exception and not the rule.

Glasses Direct is another good example of a startup that found itself in a position to be a low price leader. They sell prescription glasses directly to customers at discounts of 60%+ off the retail purchase price. They can do this because they handle the entire transaction online and through the mail. Customers send them a prescription and some additional measurements, then choose frames, and pay online. Glasses Direct delivers glasses a few days later and accepts returns gladly. Real cost savings result in a lower price while still giving them an exceptional level of profitability.

JARGON BUSTER

A *low price leader* is a business that focuses all its efforts on consistently having a low price and leads the market. They may even dip their prices below the market cost, to get the edge on their competitors.

THE PROCESS OF PERFECT PRICING

As we have discussed previously, your costs have nothing to do with the price you charge customers. All the ingredients in a bottle of Coca-Cola, the bottle itself, and all the branding on it, costs less than 10 pence.

The Coca-Cola company feels no need at all to price its product at a few pence per bottle. Sometimes this truth is explained away by pointing out how much the company spends on advertisements and maintaining its brand. The truth is, if Coca-Cola's customers decided only to pay 10 pence a bottle, Coca-Cola would change its branding and all other elements of its business model to keep profits high while meeting that requirement. And if they couldn't, they would stop producing the product.

The price people are willing to pay for a product or service can be derived from many factors and will vary from person to person and from day to day.

A person stuck in the rain on the way to a business meeting will pay quite a bit for an umbrella. Someone who buys plane tickets online will almost always want to spend less than someone who buys those tickets from a travel agent.

Some factors that customers may take into account when figuring out how much they will pay for something, include:

JARGON BUSTER

Your *value proposition* is your promise to deliver value to your customer and your customer's trust that they are getting real value.

- **The problem-solving nature of a product or service:** A commuter spending £100 and two hours getting to work every day will find spending £250 a month on a new car reasonable.
- **The long-term investment of a product or service:** This is the amount of money the customer can earn by owning a given product or using a given service. Buying a £1000 high-speed printer makes a lot of sense if you can use it to produce books that you can sell for £20 each.
- **The status derived from owning or using a product or service:** When you work in sales, having a Rolex watch might be a sign that you're a successful sales professional and that you expect to be paid a top salary.
- **The improved self-esteem from using a product or service:** A woman who spends £100 to get a great haircut because it makes her feel like a million dollars.
- **The crisis averted by using a product or service:** Spending £20 on fire alarms makes a lot of sense if buying them stops your house from burning down.
- **The need or desire that is fulfilled, on an ongoing basis:** Someone can spend £100 on a steam cleaner to use again and again or £100 every six months on a professional steam-cleaning carpet service.

- **The price paid for related products and services:** If someone spends £350 on their tablet computer, they'll not want to spend just £3 on a flimsy cover.
- **The location where the product or service is being provided:** People will pay more for a drink on holiday than in their local pub.
- **Who will be using the product or service:** People spend a lot of money on clothing for children because they love their children and the money they spend is one of the ways they express that love.
- **The customer service provided post-sale:** People will spend more for a watch that comes with a lifetime warranty than for one that is sold without a guarantee.
- **The pre-sales support required to lead customers to the best solution for their needs:** People will spend more on a bespoke suit than a suit off the rack.

You can choose to target customers based on any of these characteristics and direct your marketing efforts toward customers who do relatively little in the way of comparison shopping.

You might need to adjust the products and services you offer, to address the needs of these less 'price sensitive' customers.

For example, the cost of getting a tow truck to pick up a broken-down car may be just £20. But a roadside assistance service that guarantees to rescue a stranded daughter in the middle of the night on a dark road is worth paying £250. If your objective is to sell tow truck services, you should obviously consider modifying your business model to provide the more profitable solution. After all, many people purchase roadside assistance service plans but few use them even once a year.

Good pricing requires good market research. Look for people who are ideal customers for your product. You need to understand how they think, get under their skin, and give them what they want. When you can do that, you won't need to compete on price. You'll be able to compete on everything else.

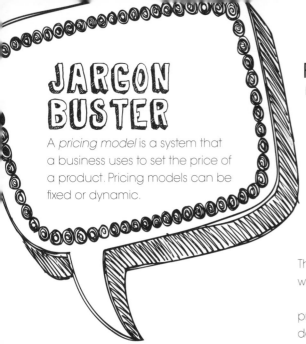

A *pricing model* is a system that a business uses to set the price of a product. Pricing models can be fixed or dynamic.

Understanding pricing models

DYNAMIC PRICING

Dynamic pricing models allow the price to vary based on the cost of resources, competitor prices or buyer negotiation. Prices may change by the minute, the hour, the month, or with every sale. The cost of lobster in a fancy restaurant may vary depending on the kind of season the fishermen had or the weight of the lobster, so the price on the menu may be dynamic.

FIXED PRICING

Fixed prices are set and remain the same for a long period of time. For example, a bottle of Chanel No.5 might cost £70 this year and it will probably cost £70 next year simply because it's a price that Chanel customers expect to pay. Moving the price up or down would make buyers wonder, 'Am I getting the best price for this bottle of perfume?' That's not a question that Chanel wants its customers to ask.

The method you use to set your prices on an ongoing basis will depend on what your customers expect and what your business requires to cover its costs. As you learn more about pricing models you may find one or more method that fits your business and is common to your industry. It's not uncommon for a business to have multiple pricing models that evolve over time.

FEATURE DEPENDENT PRICING

This pricing strategy requires you to compare your product, feature by feature, with similar products sold by your competitors. Essentially you'll come up with a percentage of the price that'll be associated with each feature. You can then give your customer a price sheet, or menu, that lets them get the product they want by selecting a set of features. A hair salon uses this strategy when it lets you buy a simple haircut and then add a conditioning treatment, a colour revamp or a blow dry. The price for each 'feature' that customers can buy is usually set, but the price they pay overall, will vary.

CUSTOMER SEGMENT DEPENDENT PRICING

This pricing model calculates what each segment of a given target market will pay, to get the service it desires. Hotels and concierge services that offer a 'Standard' service and a 'Platinum' service are pricing their services based on who their customers think they are and what they are willing to pay to get the level of attention they desire. Some customers will just uniformly choose 'Platinum service' even when they aren't sure what specific benefits they're receiving. They just want to be treated better than everyone else, to the greatest extent possible!

AUCTION PRICING

This pricing model is based on presenting a given product or service to a group of potential customers and allowing them to dynamically set the price, through bidding. This is a great way to set a price when you have something many people want but not everyone can buy. Estate jewellery and fine art are often purchased through an auction process. Sites like eBay make this auction pricing easy.

MARKET PRICING

This pricing model is used to set the price of a commonly available product or service based on the average price charged by a large number of competitors. When a restaurant says its lobster is 'market priced', it means that the price is set at a small amount above the price the restaurant pays to buy the lobster on the open market. Gold and silver is priced this way as well.

VOLUME OR MODERATION DEPENDENT PRICING

In this category the price of a product or service varies depending how much the customer buys. Washing powder is a good example. If you buy a small box of washing powder you'll pay more per unit of powder than if you buy a big box of washing powder. It becomes cheaper the more you buy.

RETAIL PRICING

Retail pricing is about setting the price of your product or service in such a way that you can compensate stores and other resellers for selling it for you.

Let's take a moment to consider ladies' handbags and how to price products for resale through retail stores. Generally speaking, the stuff these bags are made of varies little and the cost of the materials used to create them is fairly

standard, globally. But that doesn't stop Fendi and Fiorelli selling handbags at vastly different prices. Retail pricing is dependent on who you sell your product *to* and who you sell it *through*. The distribution chain is dependent on the target market you're trying to reach.

When you sell to luxury customers through premium department stores, a percentage of each sale goes to the department store for stocking, selling, delivering and accepting returns for the product. This means the price of your product will have to be set fairly high. When a reseller opens a shop on Regent Street, it's a social signal. It says, 'My handbags are so expensive that I can put one in a shop on Regent Street and the cost of the handbag will cover the whole cost of getting it there and the cost of it sitting in a shop that costs a huge amount of rent, where it's virtually the only item in the shop. That's how exclusive and expensive my handbag is...'. High-end shops don't want to carry low-cost products because their fancy customers won't buy them.

When you sell through retailers that cater to less affluent target markets, your price is lower because that's what the target market wants to pay. The shop takes a percentage of this lower price, and you get the rest. Retail pricing varies from store to store, but generally speaking resellers keep 20% to 40% of the retail purchase price of a product.

A QUICK WORD ON RETAIL PRICING AND EXCHANGE RATES

If your product or service is based on resources that you import from other countries, remember to take into account the exchange rate. Say you buy a component of your product for 50p and the exchange rate increases the price to £2. Suddenly you have a product or service that costs a lot more to deliver. If you've offered a long-term, fixed price to your resellers, this change in exchange rate could put you out of business. You'd be obligated to deliver a product you can't afford to produce.

The way around this is to fix the amount that you'll pay in pounds in all of your deals with suppliers so that the exchange rate becomes the supplier's problem. The same goes for when you work with resellers, whether in the UK or overseas – fix the amount they pay you, in pounds. If you can't do that, put a clause in the deal that lets you refund a reseller's money in order to step out of the contract without the risk of being sued. There are many other ways to handle this exchange rate risk, but the two mentioned here are probably the easiest to understand and put into practice.

GET YOUR HANDS DIRTY

Try this: Choose a pricing model or models to maximize your profits.

1. Consider each of the revenue models we've mentioned and think about what you want to sell. Which model or models will work best for you? Every business can package its value to customers in any number of ways and making the right choice of revenue model can be the difference between failure and success.

2. Based on the revenue models you want to pursue, create a list of competing products and services from other providers.

3. Record the price of each competing product in each channel through which you want to sell.

4. Consider the pricing model each competitor employs. Is their pricing fixed or dynamic? Is it feature-dependent, market segment dependent, set by auction?

5. Next to each product, record the advantages that each product – and its associated pricing and revenue – offer to the customer.

6. Add your product to the list and record the advantages that it offers to you and your customers, relative to the competition.

7. Based on the advantages that your product has, relative to competing products, calculate the range within which your product's price must be set. This will be based on what you've learned from your research. If that price is not high enough to cover your per unit costs, you'll have to either increase the value of your product to customers, lower your production costs, or change to another revenue model that will make a profit.

8. Create one or more financial forecasts until you're certain you have chosen a pricing model and a revenue model that will maximize profit.

Something to note here is that you can use this method to find a price for products that haven't yet been created. You can test the theory or showcase the prototype. Define the product, compare its anticipated advantages to what is currently on the market, and then present your prototype product or service to customers with prices that are in line with the value and advantages you provide. Adjust your pricing as you begin pitching your product to see the point at which people start wanting to place orders.

Using financial forecasts to calculate profits based on prices, revenue and costs

The art of financial forecasting is probably the only technical skill that every entrepreneur needs to have true competence in, in order to run their business profitably. Unfortunately it's the one creatives fear the most. If we strip away all the noise and the nonsense you hear about how scary financial forecasting is, it's simply addition, subtraction, multiplication and division. With the aid of a calculator, you'll be able to make a cash flow forecast stand up and dance by the time I'm done with this chapter.

STEP-BY-STEP INSTRUCTIONS FOR CREATING A CASH FLOW FORECAST

The following instructions will help you create a forecast of your cash flow for any given period of time. You can use this as you start and grow your business, to keep track of how much you're spending and how much you're earning. It'll help you determine, in advance, when problems with cash flow will be dangerous to your business.

JARGON BUSTER

A *financial forecast* is the evidence written in numbers of the plan for your business. It's simply saying, if I stand here today and look forward from where my business is right now, what happens next? As described in pounds and pence.

CASHFLOW

	INITIAL INVESTMENT	week 1	week 2	week 3	week 4
BEGINNING CASH	£1000.00	£1000.00	£805.00	£830.00	£855.00
FIXED COSTS					
Founder Compensation		800.00	800.00	800.00	800.00
Employee Compensation		400.00	400.00	400.00	400.00
Phones		20.00	20.00	20.00	20.00
Internet		50.00	50.00	50.00	50.00
Website Hosting		5.00	5.00	5.00	5.00
Travel		100.00	100.00	100.00	100.00
Rented Space		100.00	100.00	100.00	100.00
Business Insurance		1000.00	1000.00	1000.00	1000.00
Legal Expenses		200.00	200.00	200.00	200.00
VARIABLE COSTS THAT CHANGE BASED ON THE WORK WE DO					
Contractor Compensation		200.00	200.00	200.00	200.00
Cost of Raw Materials & Resources		300.00	300.00	300.00	300.00
Production & Packaging Costs		50.00	50.00	50.00	50.00
Commissions		50.00	50.00	50.00	50.00
Marketing Costs (events, tradeshows, ads)		75.00	75.00	75.00	75.00
Advertising Costs (Google ads, Facebook ads, etc.)		75.00	75.00	75.00	75.00
Shipping Costs		20.00	20.00	20.00	20.00
Tax Payments		100.00	100.00	100.00	100.00
INCOME					
Money Received from Direct Sales through Website		700.00	700.00	700.00	700.00
Money Received from Consignment Sales		1000.00	1000.00	1000.00	1000.00
Money Received from Distributors		800.00	800.00	800.00	800.00
Royalties from Licensing Agreement		900.00	900.00	900.00	900.00
ENDING CASH	£1000.00	£805.00	£830.00	£855.00	£880.00

1. Open a spreadsheet and call it 'Cash Flow'.

2. Create a row called 'Beginning Cash'. The amount of money your business has in the bank each week goes in this column.

3. Next, list your expenses. Put in the fixed costs that you always have to pay. This could be office rent, salaries, insurance and so on.

4. Now list the costs that vary, based on what you do. These could be the costs for raw materials, packing supplies, advertising and so on.

5. Make a list of the ways the company earns income, for example direct sales, consignment or distribution.

6. Put in a 'Total' row that sums up all the figures in each column and tells you if you make a profit or loss. This is your 'Ending Cash' amount. If your business makes a profit every week, you'll make a profit for the year.

7. If, in any given week, the Total Profit or Loss value is negative, that is a week the company is losing money, you need to find a way to increase revenue or reduce costs that week.

8. Save your spreadsheet and update it once or twice a week to reflect the changes in costs and revenues over time.

HOW DO YOU MAKE GOOD FINANCIAL ASSUMPTIONS?

How do you know that the guesses or assumptions you make about your business's financial future are correct – or at least, as close as you can get them? Start by laying out all that you know about your business at this point. Usually this means all the costs, with little or no sales. This is the hurdle your business must jump each month. It is known as the *burn rate* of the business.

I usually memorise the monthly burn rate number and divide it into how much per week and per day it costs to run my business. I literally break it down to see how much I spend per day. How much does my business cost per day? Imagine it costs £1,000 a day to keep my business open, which are my core costs with overheads and salary included. I sell an item for £2,000 one day when I'm out selling and I make a

gross profit. That means I've just bought my business one more day of existence. This is known as the *ramp*.

In the US they use the term *runway* to describe a startup's cash flow in the early days. They compare a startup to a plane going down the runway with a certain amount of fuel (cash in the bank). If the startup doesn't have enough capital to stay in business because its burn rate is too high or its initial capital is too low, the plane will crash.

In the earliest days of your business, you'll be investing your time and the few pounds you have to get your business off the ground. If you can create a product that practically sells itself to a clearly defined, fast-growing, target market, you'll have minimized your burn rate and given yourself a long runway. In fact, you might never run out of ramp. If you've followed the instructions outlined in this book you're well on your way to creating such a magical product.

JARGON BUSTER

The *ramp* or *run time* or *run time to exhaustion* is how much time you have before you run out of money.

JARGON BUSTER

Burn rate is the amount of money you 'burn' or 'burn through' if you don't sell anything and nothing happens with your business (no sales, no investment, no movement). It's a measure of how fast – the rate – at which a small company will use up its capital.

BOOTSTRAP BUDGETING

There are only two ways to make money in business – grow the revenue or decrease the cost. The only thing you can control is the cost. You can only hope for increased revenue.

Keeping your overheads to a minimum early on is an absolute must. Avoiding things like an office and opting instead to work at home or in a shared workspace is an easy way to save money. Starting out with a simple website that you can build yourself rather than paying a wad of cash for an all-singing, all-dancing website is more cost-effective. There are thousands of ways to keep your costs low and to be work-smart. Other people have done some of the hard graft in designing apps and services that will ease your workload and reduce your outgoings. Simple research will open up a whole world of cost-effective resources to you.

JARGON BUSTER

Bootstrap budgeting means keeping your costs as lean as possible and spending sparingly.

My best advice for you is, try not to spend unnecessarily. Ideally, you want to be running a very lean business. The money you spend now that you don't have, becomes a debt that you acquire and a burden that you carry. A business that costs very little floats up gently into profit and success.

GET YOUR HANDS DIRTY

Try this: For those selling through resellers, check that the distributor and reseller's pricing of your products will cover your costs.

1. Calculate your cost per unit of production including manufacturing, packing, shipping, handling, etc.
2. Calculate the Minimum Price to Distributors as twice this cost.
3. Calculate the Minimum Price to the Customer (retail price) as three times this cost.
4. If your product's advantages do not justify this price to the customer, look at the advantages delivered by all the other products and services that compete with what you offer. Try to work out which would be the most cost-effective to add to your offering, to justify a higher price.

GROW

SHRINK

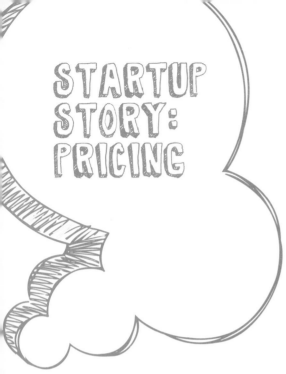

STARTUP STORY: PRICING

SAUL KLEIN

FOUNDER, VIDEO ISLAND, FORERUNNER TO LOVEFILM

www.lovefilm.com

Saul Klein founded Video Island, one of the three startups that, after a number of mergers and acquisitions, became LoveFilm – now the premier online film rental and streaming service in the UK and around Europe. Saul remained on the board at LoveFilm until it was sold to Amazon in 2011. He is a partner at venture firm Index Ventures and is co-founder of Seedcamp.

At the time Video Island launched, there were the other startups – Online Rentals Ltd and ScreenSelect – there was the incumbent, Blockbuster, and the threat of the innovator – Netflix – which was active only in the US. There was also the threat of other companies coming into the market as they had done in the US. One of my concerns was actually less about the other startups and more about companies like Tesco coming into the market. In the US, Walmart had launched their own DVD online rental service and they were the largest retailer of DVDs globally. I knew Tesco were smart enough to be tracking Walmart, I knew how big Tesco was as a retailer and how much they wanted to grow their non-food category. At the time, music and movies were the ways to grow and DVDs, like CDs, are great to sell at retail because

they don't take up much shelf space.

I was concerned that Tesco was coming into the market and I thought they would be more challenging to compete with than Blockbuster; Tesco have 1,700 stores in the UK, are the biggest brand in the UK and have more buying power than Blockbuster. From a strategy perspective, I decided to focus less on building a direct-to-consumer brand because I felt that if we were successful as a business, we would be able to build a brand later down the line. There's always that anxiety when you pitch to big companies but my feeling was that when I walked into the meeting with Tesco my best-case scenario would be that they saw value in this service and they would want to work with us. My fallback was they saw value in the service but they didn't want to work with us. In that case, we

would just go to the next supermarket down. My worst-case scenario was that they just wouldn't care because then I wouldn't have had anyone to help me fight Blockbuster or Amazon.

When you introduce a new category to consumers, it's a very expensive exercise. Back then, people were used to going to their local video shop and that's how they thought about renting movies, or they bought a DVD cheaply at Tesco or at petrol stations. My view was that if we could persuade big brands to work with us – a big retailer, a big media company, a big online company – then we could leverage these brands to do the job of educating the market and building awareness for us. Strategically we would then be able to go to the film studios and instead of saying, 'Hey, we're a company you've never heard of...', we could say, 'Hey, we're Video Island and we're running DVD rental services for B2B retailers and media companies that you know and do business with, so what price are you going to give us?'. Our market entry strategy was basically geared around the defensive aspects: I wanted someone on my side who would be bigger than Blockbuster and had more reach than Blockbuster and more supplier clout than Blockbuster. My fundamental belief from an offensive angle was that it takes a long time to build a business and we would be able to learn by working with established partners. We could find out which customer acquisition channels were effective, what pricing worked... and even better, it was all being tested on their dollar, not on our dollar.

I knew there would be a time when, if consumers genuinely liked these propositions, we would be able to invest in our own brand and there would be a ready market for us to move into. We went out and we tried to target the biggest retailer, the biggest media owner, the biggest online company and also someone who was prepared to do something innovative. We were lucky in that the first partner that came on board was Tesco and that was the real validation that we had something to offer. I knew that if we could keep Tesco happy – which is not easy – but if we could, we would learn an enormous amount from them; and we did. We learned about unit economics, managing a weekly Profit & Loss, operational efficiency, tweaking

propositions, e-mail effectiveness, direct mail, in-store selling... the list goes on. We were very open in the deal that we did with Tesco because of how validating it was to our business just to have them on board. I wasn't so fussed about branding and developing our own brand. I knew if we had Tesco as a partner then Blockbuster wouldn't bother us and Netflix wouldn't bother us. I became more aware Amazon might be a competitor and that was the one company that Tesco saw as their main competitor. We had on our side this big brother in Tesco, which could crush any of the so-called big guns out there. That was a very successful relationship.

We got ITV on the media side which was the biggest commercial broadcaster. It didn't turn out to be a very good partnership. It built credibility but in terms of building customers, Tesco was more useful. On the online side, at the time MSN was the largest online portal. We built MSN DVD online rental with them. They had more traffic to MSN.com than any other site in the UK. We had a link on that same page and I think for the first time, our servers went down. But the conversion rates were pathetic. It wasn't targeted and it was sold in a way that was less effective than Tesco. There was lots of awareness but very low conversions. Another strategic avenue was cinemas and we ended up working with VUE Cinemas.

The key proposition for LoveFilm was actually innovated by Netflix, and was based on the premise that you could use the Internet to do a few things:

1. Give people 50 times the selection that they could get at the normal video shop.
2. Offer the convenience to the customer of creating a film list and be able to instantly access that list of movies that they had chosen.
3. Send stuff through the mail and not worry about postage because it was free – removing the hassle and offering convenience.
4. Remove the penalty for enjoying the product. Blockbuster used to make some ridiculous percentage of profit on late fees. We basically wanted to be good to the consumer and say, 'Keep it as long as you like, we don't care; when you've finished, send it back'. That was an amazing value proposition.
5. Offer a free trial: more selection convenience, no penalty fee and no ongoing commitment that trapped the customer.

With LoveFilm, the price point started at £14.99 for three DVDs a month, which, versus Sky Movies or going to the cinema or to Blockbuster, was an attractive and competitive proposition. Successful consumer propositions have to work on multiple levels. They have to be rational and emotional. From a rational perspective the things that appeal are choice and convenience. On the emotional level the tension-inducing relationship of the late fee was a killer. Once you've hooked someone rationally and emotionally, and then you give them the ability to try at no cost, that's an awesome proposition.

In e-commerce, you have selection, convenience and price. They are always the three propositions that online businesses have to nail. Our innovation was our go-to-market strategy, in working with these big brands to build awareness to do proposition testing. Only at that point did we go out and start investing significantly in LoveFilm as a brand. The pricing that we tested, we did with Stelios (the entrepreneur and owner of easyJet). We did easyDVD rental. We saw that the subscription model had had success in the US but I think we were concerned that £14.99

was quite a lot of money for something new and unproven. If you're a heavy consumer of entertainment, maybe, but for the average person who might only watch one or two movies a month it was expensive. We innovated in pricing the year before Netflix actually, in that we brought our introductory package down from £14.99 and, inspired by Tesco, hit the price point of £9.99 for two DVDs a month. Our customer could upgrade to three DVDs but what we sold was the £9.99 package. It's obvious but you'd have to be a retailer to see quite how obvious it was; lead with your strongest price point, accessible to the largest number of people. Netflix was slavishly doing £14.99 for three DVDs, and whether they looked at us and followed suit or just came to the same conclusion as us I don't know, but both LoveFilm and Netflix over time moved to a lower and lower price point. At certain points we also tested £4.99 a month for one DVD at a time.

The test with Stelios was as close to the model of going into the retail store – the model the customer understood – as possible. It was £1.99 for one movie. That actually wasn't a bad proposition – it worked for Stelios. The way I rationalise it is that in the mobile phone market there is contract and there is pre-pay. Not everyone in the UK wants to have a contract or, in this case, a subscription. So we tried to create a 'pre-paid' equivalent in movie rental, where the customer could purchase a pack of ten rentals, charged on an individual basis.

Glasses Direct (www.glassesdirect.

co.uk) is another company that I'm involved with and the founder's insight there was essentially that the average pair of glasses on the high street cost £150 but it's possible to sell glasses online for £15, which is how much it costs to make them. The margins that Specsavers et al are making are egregious. Glasses Direct had a very powerful initial proposition but the challenge was that you can't actually make money over time selling £15 glasses. Over the years when we invested in Glasses Direct the average basket value was £34; it's now around the £80 or £90 mark. It's still amazing value, with way more selection than the high street, more convenient because you can shop anytime you like. People want their spouse or friend or partner to give their opinion on their glasses so Glasses Direct offer four trial pairs of glasses to try at home, which no optician on the high street would do. All three elements are critically important – selection, convenience and pricing – and then comes the context of how to profitably sell this product or service. You need to sell at a decent margin or else you won't be in business long.

I've worked at companies like Microsoft and eBay, Skype and Ogilvy and I've never seen a big company that can compete with a small company that's focused and determined and knows what they're doing. And if they can and do try to compete with your small startup then great, but you know what? They've got three or four competitors, so go and work with them. Have a conversation with their competitors – it's way easier. It was always part of the original plan to be the gateway to light entertainment. We knew we would never do just what Netflix did. We thought we might do games and music and we understood that when the infrastructure was ready from the broadband side and the device side we would love to stream or distribute digitally because our biggest cost was postage. Had we remained a standalone business, we would've looked very similar to what the Kindle Fire is offering – a hardware bundle with entertainment – but it would've been subscription-based with a Spotify-like music service and games service, possibly a magazines and books service. Ultimately that would be the domain of Amazon, who bought the company and had a lot of assets to bring to the table.

Apple weren't really on the horizon when we were starting the business and since then obviously everyone from Google to Microsoft and every media company and telco in the world wants to be in this business as well, which is ultimately what makes it a very expensive business to be in. Google doesn't stand still; Tesco doesn't stand still; BP doesn't stand still. That's just good business.

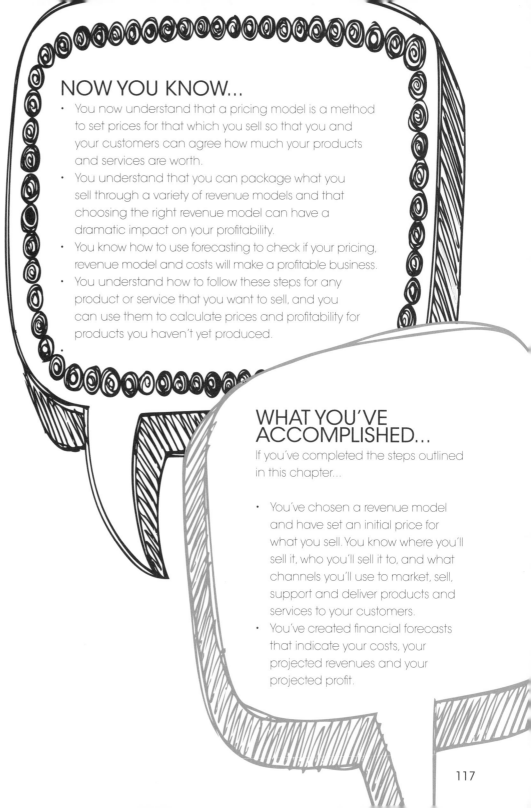

NOW YOU KNOW...

- You now understand that a pricing model is a method to set prices for that which you sell so that you and your customers can agree how much your products and services are worth.
- You understand that you can package what you sell through a variety of revenue models and that choosing the right revenue model can have a dramatic impact on your profitability.
- You know how to use forecasting to check if your pricing, revenue model and costs will make a profitable business.
- You understand how to follow these steps for any product or service that you want to sell, and you can use them to calculate prices and profitability for products you haven't yet produced.

WHAT YOU'VE ACCOMPLISHED...

If you've completed the steps outlined in this chapter...

- You've chosen a revenue model and have set an initial price for what you sell. You know where you'll sell it, who you'll sell it to, and what channels you'll use to market, sell, support and deliver products and services to your customers.
- You've created financial forecasts that indicate your costs, your projected revenues and your projected profit.

CHAPTER 8: THE KEY PARTNER

WHO IS OUR KEY PARTNER?

WHO IS OUR KEY PARTNER?

Every startup has one or more partners that become critical to their success. These might be suppliers that give terms to a new business, distributors that take on a new product very early in its life cycle, or marketing partners that present your company and its offerings to more customers than you could pay to reach. Knowing who your key partners are, or need to be, can make building your company much easier because you'll know which relationships are the most important and why.

The primary value of a partnership is the *leverage* it gives you. The point of this question is to help you look at various partners and measure them on their potential for *leverage*.

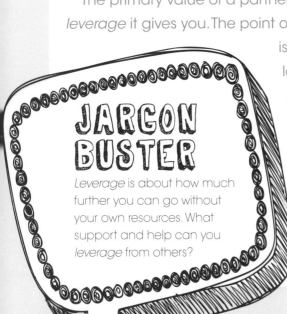

JARGON BUSTER

Leverage is about how much further you can go without your own resources. What support and help can you *leverage* from others?

The reason 'Key Partner' has become one of my Ten Questions is because the inherent egotism of being an entrepreneur makes you misjudge not just the size of your business but your potential aspiration... and when I say misjudge, I mean completely, utterly miss the mark. Startup founders misunderstand the size of their business, the size of the world and the relationship of one to the other. They see businesses that are a magnitude larger than their own business and think they are close in size.

This is a little humbling, but a necessary reality check:

> In your first year of trading if you're fortunate, you might sell £50,000–£100,000 worth of goods.
> If you grow 10 times and hit a million pounds, you're still a micro-business.
> If you have a 1000% increase in sales, you're still a micro-business.
> If you have another 1000% increase in sales, you're creeping into the next category of SME (small to medium enterprise).

I use those statements not to intimidate you but just to help you understand how much distance there is, to get to 'big'. Startups overlook the power of a large partner because they underestimate the reach those partners have that their startup simply doesn't have and can't create overnight.

SOME TRUTHS ABOUT KEY PARTNERS

- Partners can help with the cost to capital or risk, or cost of marketing.
- Partners can create immediate customers or access to customers that you couldn't, or distribution channels that you wouldn't otherwise be able to create.
- Partners give access to the inaccessible.
- Partners can solve the problems of a small business – and not just the small problems but the big

uglies like finding capital, reaching customers, reaching your target market, getting access to distribution channels.
- Partners are part of the critical path to success.
- Partners increase the odds of success tremendously and should be treated as one of the most important things you achieve early on.
- If you get the partner on board early, your business will grow faster.

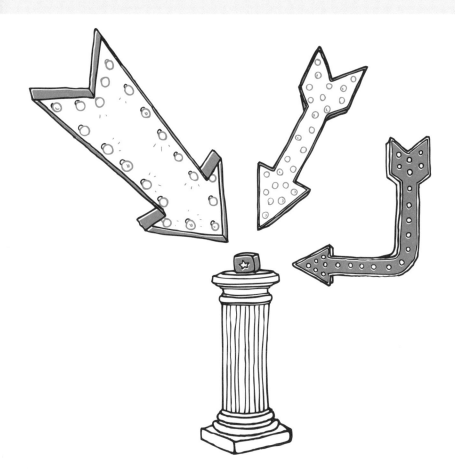

A MARKETING OR VISIBILITY PARTNER

New business owners often misunderstand the value of visibility. They drastically underestimate how much it costs to contact their target market through advertising, social networks or editorial content. If you find a partner who can help you reach a huge number of people in your target market with the right information about your wonderful product or service, you will have a much greater chance of closing sales and becoming very profitable.

Learning how to find and work with visibility partners is one of the most important skills you can master. If you really understand your target market, you should be able to help anyone who shares that target market benefit by working with you.

If you can identify a company that reaches your target market day-in, day-out, then you should forge a relationship with them that lets them deliver something you've designed. They can introduce you to potentially millions of customers, almost overnight. It might be worth designing and licensing something exclusive that only that visibility partner has a right to sell.

Why would a large, well-connected enterprise be willing to work with your young business? Because you are delivering a benefit to their customers that they would otherwise find impossible to deliver. While not every marketing partner will be interested in your plan, you only need one to say yes to gain a tremendous amount of visibility.

1. Look for one or more businesses that routinely interact with your target market.
2. Identify how your startup can provide a product or service that helps this partner achieve an important business objective. Can you help them close more sales? Get repeat business? Provide better support to their customers?
3. Think about how much it would cost you to help their business.
4. Write down your strategy, your game plan, for how this will work.
5. Contact the senior marketing executive at the selected business and pitch your plan to him/her. Include your cost for providing this service. Reach out to them via a phone call or email. You could use LinkedIn and target the Director of Marketing or the CEO. When you do get someone on the phone, find out if they like what you're proposing and if not, why not. Learning about your customer from a sale that fails is the easiest way to increase future sales.
6. Contact ten to twelve folks this way. If you don't get interest you don't have a good understanding of the people you're approaching or their target market.

GET YOUR HANDS DIRTY

Try this: Look for a marketing partner that can offer you visibility.

BUSINESS SENSITIVITY

Ask yourself, what's critical in your business? Technically this is called a 'business sensitivity'. The business is 'sensitive' to the peril – or the profit – from that point in the business.

At School for Creative Startups, we had a student whose most critical partner was his glass-blowing manufacturer because of the uniqueness of his work and the kind of specialist skills that were required to make it. There was seemingly only one manufacturing partner who could produce his goods to the right specification and quality. This was partly an industry issue in that the glass-blowing skills required weren't in abundance and partly that his designs were so specialised and intricate that it had to be someone very skilled who could take on the task. Our student therefore had a *critical path partner* and he needed to keep that partner happy.

If your business only stays in business because you've got great terms with a given supplier, you need to realise that supplier is your de facto partner and you have to ensure you're meeting the supplier's needs over time.

A SUPPLIER PARTNER

This is a potential partnership that startups tend to overlook. In most instances, startups see suppliers just as suppliers, but supplier partners can be the making of a company. If suppliers believe in you they can extend your credit earlier and reduce your cost of capital dramatically.

Suppliers can offer support and access to contacts; they can become a centre of gravity for the manufacture of what you're doing. Suppliers can help the product itself if they have a design team. They might know how to build something that's better quality and cheaper to produce. Think about what they could do for you, stimulate their trust, win them over and learn what they can bring to the table. In each instance of a partnership there is a reason why those partners will find *you* valuable.

In the case of a supplier partner, if it's a manufacturer and you are only

JARGON BUSTER

A *critical path partner* is a partner that is critical to the business being able to function.

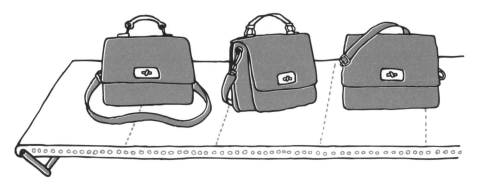

buying a small number of goods, you might wonder why they would be keen to work with you. If you're asking a leather manufacturer who stitches together tens of thousands of handbags a year to create 50 lovely samples of handbags for you, why would the manufacturer be interested in such a small order? Quite simply, most manufacturing companies, especially factories, are built to go to capacity and need to run near full capacity all the time. They also know that their longest standing customers started out small and grew over time, organically.

Manufacturers are always hoping that the next small business that knocks on their door is going to be a long-term customer. When you make the approach to a manufacturer they don't just see you as a small customer with a small order; they see your potential. Your 50 sample handbags could become 50,000 handbags over the coming years and if you have confidence in the story you tell, if you create a vision they can buy into and if you act like a potential long-term customer, they can see you morph into a

potentially important client. Remember when we talked about practising the patter and storytelling in Chapter 1? This is the occasion to use it. If you believe in your product, if you have evidence in the marketplace, if you have retailers that are interested in what you do, tell the supplier your story.

A FINANCE PARTNER
Technically known as a supply finance partner, these guys deal with one of the many issues you have when starting out which is that if you're

JARGON BUSTER

A special instance of supply finance is known as *Purchase Order Finance*. This is when you have an order from a customer and you can show the purchase order as evidence of the customer's order, even though there isn't any money attached to it.

making something, you need to have some cash in hand to send to the manufacturer as a deposit before they will make the goods. Manufacturers are unlikely to extend any credit to you at the beginning and, if they are feeling generous, they will only ask for part of the money upfront and part of the money on completion. Even on completion, as a startup you only have inventory (the product) and no profit from sales, so that's why you might need supply finance.

With Purchase Order Finance, a partner will give you the money to produce the goods on the evidence that you have an order and you just need to create the product, sell it and invoice the customer to pay that money back to the partner.

If you can find someone willing enough to work with you on that financial aspect, ideally on a long-term basis where you can build trust and credit with that partner over time, this could be the key to making your business grow. This works well if you have lots of distribution channels eager for your product. Many small businesses think small because they intuitively know that they have no money. You probably wouldn't think small if you knew you had lots of stores waiting for your product, lots of distribution channels and someone lending you the money to create your goods! You live inside walls that you create. I'm challenging you to climb the wall.

A DISTRIBUTOR PARTNER

A lot of young companies think distributors just take money to ship goods to a store and that they could do the job just as easily themselves.

Distributors have other qualities that you need to appreciate. Firstly, they can offer credit to their customers (retailers) on your behalf. They have an existing relationship with their customers – the retailers – that you don't. Secondly, customers don't want to buy from a number of different manufacturers, they want to place one order from one company to get all of their goods from one distribution point. Thirdly, the distributor can hold your stock for you, take calls at night, ship items overnight and do all of the ugly logistics that you can't do as well. They can offer convenience and effortlessness. Distributors make it easy. They make selection and paying for goods relatively painless.

Why would a distributor want to work with a little startup like you? Because the distributors' biggest challenge is that they don't have a reason to call their customer (the retailers). They make up promotions endlessly as an excuse to engage with their customer, the retailer. They need a reason to call their retailers and that reason could be your company, your wonderful, distinct product and your newness. You can keep their product line fresh.

Every distributor wants to avoid the peril of being undifferentiated and anonymous. If they are distributing your products they can borrow some of your panache, they can share some of your brand glory. If you're interesting, they're interesting; if you're distinct and memorable, they're distinct and memorable. Distributors can create bundles of products, which are unique packages of products at the point of distribution, from many manufacturers. These are bundles that are entirely unique to them.

When I go to a distributor, I always say to them, 'Let me tell you how I can help you guys make more sales'. Don't begrudge the margin the distributor makes from you; support them thoroughly and remind yourself that they want you as much as you want them.

A SERVICE PARTNER

A product rarely sits alone in the world. Almost all products have a context and serve a purpose when paired with something else. A decanter isn't a product that sits alone, it was designed to be used with wine.

Services tend to sit on top of products and add value to products in one way or another. They either teach or encourage the use of the product or they help to integrate it or make it work with other things. Services adjoin products perfectly, like wine tasting. A customer better educated about wine from going to wine-tasting classes will be willing to spend more money, more regularly, at the local wine merchant. In this example, the service is wine-tasting, the product is wine (and all the paraphernalia that goes with wine). If you have a service, what's the product that your service can sit comfortably alongside? If you have a product, what's the service that needs it?

A WORD ON THE 'PERFECT PARTNER'

You've probably heard the old proverb that a bird in the hand is worth two in the bush. The same goes for partners. Having a partner on board is a lot better than having a perfect, theoretical partner that you're pining for but can't woo into doing business with you. There is always an element of opportunism in determining who your partner is and it might not be the partner you expected. Partnerships in business – just like in romance and love – can be surprising and inevitably unlike you ever imagined when you dreamt of your perfect partner.

In business, waiting for the perfect partner gets you nowhere because time itself is a component in success. You need to move quickly. I always think it helps to look at your own business with people behind you and people in front of you. The people behind you are your own suppliers and supply chain that reaches you; the people in front of you are your distribution and sales chains leading out to customers. There are potential partners on both sides.

STARTUP STORY: PARTNERSHIPS

DOUG RICHARD
ITAL COMPUTERS

Doug Richard founded ITAL computers with his brother in 1985. ITAL sold computer aided design, rendering and manufacturing solutions to some of the largest enterprises in Southern California. In 1991 ITAL computers was sold in a private transaction and the profits were used to found Visual Software, which produced one of the very first affordable 3D modelling and animation applications for the PC market. Doug has more than 25 years' experience founding and building technology and software ventures, both in the US and in the UK.

I ran my first company, ITAL Computers, with my brother Ken. We were resellers of high-end computer equipment which mainly consisted of workstations. This was at a time when high-res graphics and imaging in particular were becoming popular and although this was before the digitalisation of film and TV, movie posters were coming into their own as beautiful, artful, high-res images. At ITAL we became the go-to guys for graphics in Hollywood. ITAL managed to become a reseller at the centre of Hollywood, at exactly the point when computers met Hollywood for the first time. As a reseller, we were on the hunt for computers that would help us fulfil this niche market for graphics, and we found Silicon Graphics Inc. (SGI), a workstation company that did beautiful graphics.

In the early days we reached out quite aggressively to SGI and we started to sell quite a few of their computers in Hollywood because of their appeal within the industry. SGI were positive about the partnership in the beginning and actively collaborated on our strategy and exploring routes to market.

But as we developed more than just a vendor-distributor relationship it became clear to SGI just how important Hollywood was as the key industry sector that was central to their emerging sales strategy. Hollywood was too important, SGI decided, to give over to a reseller (ITAL Computers) when SGI could serve that market themselves. Or so they thought. SGI didn't see the true value of the partnership with ITAL and they were arrogant enough to think they didn't

need the skills of the reseller. Though they made great headway in the market, they were overtaken by other workstation manufacturers who worked with the reseller community and thus obtained the enormous leverage that distributors and resellers provide.

The moral of the story is this; if you're the manufacturer, never be tempted to think you're more important than your

reseller. Just because it's your product, doesn't mean it's your sale! SGI didn't need to get rid of ITAL but ITAL survived the fallout; we went to Sun Microsystems and we did wonderful things with them under the partnerships banner.

There are always potential risks with partnerships, even when there's a lot of love on both sides. There's a famous business expression – a 'bear hug' – which is when a very large company loves a very small company so much that they actually hug it to death. It gets crushed by love. In its enthusiasm, the big company doesn't understand its own size and strength and it crushes the little one.

When ITAL was trying to break into the scientific market, we were desperate for a big partner. We somehow managed to convince DEC (Digital Equipment Corporation) – at the time one of the biggest computer companies in the world – to partner with us. DEC were very excited because we were this little cutting edge business that was doing this really sharp work with animation and graphics and it was sexy stuff. They decided to put together a team to work with us but it turned out their team had more people in it than our entire company. The sheer amount of time this relationship took up could have cost my brother and me the company, if we hadn't realised early on what was happening. The effort of working with DEC probably doubled our workload. Were we rewarded by it? Hell yeah! They started giving us their 'local leads' and those local leads amounted to the whole of the Los Angeles Basin. That's a lot of leads. A small uptake for DEC was a revolution for us. We profited tremendously and grew off the back of a large corporation liking us but nevertheless we came perilously close to losing the whole company because of the effort involved in working with them and the fact that they loved us a little too much.

Recently a guy got in touch with me who had been a partner of ours back in the early days of ITAL Computers, more than 25 years ago. Our partnerships at that time were such a crucial part of the company's success that the people we worked alongside as partners are people that we still hold in high regard; people we can reach out to at any point and vice versa. A quarter of a century after we worked together and with little contact in between, I was delighted when this email from an old partner dropped into my inbox. We rode the rollercoaster together, we made money together, we toasted success together and I would still do business with him today.

Partnerships can make or break a company. The partner can be upstream or downstream of you but never underestimate their importance, their value and their power. The success of ITAL Computers was due entirely to its partnerships; it was a company that was built on and breathed partnerships. No business is profitable on its own legs, by itself.

NOW YOU KNOW...

- You understand that if your business is to thrive it must have one or more partners to help it thrive.
- You know how to find businesses to partner with and you understand the value you bring to them as a partner.
- You understand that finding a good visibility partner is key to putting your business centre stage quickly.

WHAT YOU'VE ACCOMPLISHED...

If you've completed the steps outlined in this chapter...

- You've also identified the value and strengths that your company can offer a partner.
- You've begun reaching out to these partners.

CHAPTER 9: THE ASSET

WHAT IS OUR KEY ASSET?

WHAT IS OUR KEY ASSET?

We're going to start this chapter with an activity, as it will help you understand exactly what I mean by 'asset'.

GET YOUR HANDS DIRTY
Try this: Identify your key assets.

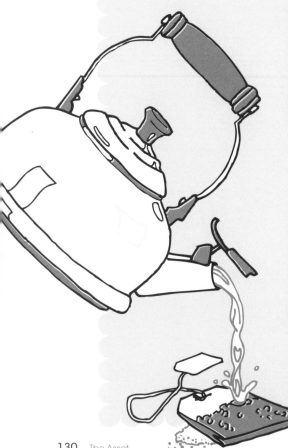

ONE

This is a chance to stop and pause for breath. Think about your answers to the previous 8 questions and take a moment to reflect on what you've discovered about your business thus far.

TWO

Now think about what single element, if taken away, would make the business difficult if not impossible to run. Note, you and your skills cannot be called an asset to your business. I'll explain why later in this chapter.

THREE

What would you buy first if you suddenly received a small investment for your business and knew the business would have to pay it back? What can you buy, that would virtually guarantee your company's success?

A company talking to customers, potential suppliers, marketing partners, investors or lenders must be able to describe its assets.

Every startup begins with assets of one kind or another. They may be the resources or contacts founders bring to the business, the ownership or existing lease of a given property, a licence to use a well-known brand name and character, or exceptional product designs owned outright.

Assets are things that you have or that you can acquire, that would make money without costing you time/hours of your life. Something that passively produces income, and something that someone could buy to produce income, are both assets.

Assets are things you own, not skills. Skills are a potential while assets are concrete, sellable things. Your employees are assets because if you sell the company they go with the business and really it's your contract for their time that you're selling. Databases are intellectual property you can sell.

You can't sell yourself as an asset, because you won't be going with the business if it's sold.

Startups create and acquire assets over time. They get new employees, contracts that provide ongoing revenue, property and cash reserves.

Generally speaking, assets fall into the following categories:

INTELLECTUAL
Copyrights, patents, trademarks, rights and licences purchased, etc.

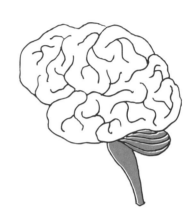

HUMAN
Expertise, name recognition, credentials, etc.

PHYSICAL
Location, equipment, inventory, etc.

FINANCIAL
Cash that's available and not invested, contracts guaranteeing future sales, revenues from licensing, etc.

Assets are an interesting topic because people always want to put themselves and their expertise down as assets, which represents a fundamental misunderstanding of both assets and how to make a living from a business.

If you're a clothing designer and you are the only one who can make the clothes you sell, in a sense you are selling your time and skill. You are limited by how much you can charge for the hours you sell. If you become ill and can't design clothes anymore, you could go out of business.

If you're a clothing designer and you create patterns and license them to folks who sell patterns to consumers, your patterns earn whether you are there or not.

If you're a clothing designer and you create patterns and hire people to make clothing based upon those patterns in your shop, your business can also make money whether you are there or not.

If you have a lease on a shop on a popular corner, and you get walk-in traffic, the leased shop is an asset because it can generate revenue whether you are there or not.

A patent, a printing press, a car, a farm... these are all assets. A list of customer names and email addresses that lets you sell new things to them again and again, that's an asset. Building the right assets, over time, makes it possible to serve more customers at a lower cost while maintaining, or even increasing, the price of what you sell. Assets, correctly chosen, make your business more profitable. So it's useful to list the assets you have and to think about the ones you need to build, and the ones you need to acquire, in order to make your company more profitable. In the process of building your business, you'll analyse customers, competitors, pricing and advantages and it will become clear that your enterprise will depend primarily on just a single asset. It may be an asset you have, or it may be something you have to acquire.

KNOW YOUR ASSET

We can look at the asset in reference to my old company Library House, which I talked about in Chapter 1 under *The Proposition*. In not knowing our proposition and thinking that our customers were buying access to the Library House database not the events, we had misidentified our asset. We thought our asset was the database but our asset was actually the events or rather, our convening capability. It was our ability to bring together into one room people who would not normally or easily congregate. If we apply question 2 above to the Library House model and ask what we could have thrown away, then we could have thrown away the database and still kept our customers happy. We couldn't have thrown away the events because we wouldn't have had any customers left!

At Library House we had a staff of 50, of which 40 were PhD researchers building a database that nobody gave a crap about! So it pains me to say this but we could have had a core team of just 10 staff running slick events, hanging out, drinking champagne, and still been wildly successful.

If you know your proposition and you know your asset, you know your value to anyone, whether a customer or a partner.

Economic replacement values

If you want to value something but it's tricky to put a price on it, you need to ask from an economical viewpoint, what would happen if it disappeared. What space would it leave in the world? Can you come up with a cost for that loss?

I was once asked to value the entirety of the University of Cambridge's contribution to the globe, to put a number on it. We did it by looking at economic replacement values, finding those things that the University of Cambridge did that weren't replicated and couldn't be reproduced elsewhere. All the stuff that could be done by others we disregarded and then we tried to cost up the stuff that was unique to the University of Cambridge and that would be an irreplaceable loss. We couldn't get close to a single number because it's impossible to find absolute values, but what we totted up was a fairly hefty figure and allowed Cambridge to talk about their contribution to the world with some form of economic evidence.

STARTUP STORY: THE ASSET

FRASER DOHERTY
FOUNDER, SUPERJAM
www.superjam.co.uk

Fraser Doherty started his business when he was just a teenager. His brand of jam – SuperJam™ – is a range of 100% pure fruit jams stocked in supermarkets such as Waitrose, Sainsbury's and Morrisons. The company has gone on to sell millions of jars, has won a variety of awards and is even exhibited in the National Museum of Scotland as an example of an 'Iconic Scottish Food Brand'. SuperJam Tea Parties (a Registered Charity) organises hundreds of free tea parties all over the UK for elderly people who live alone or in care.

About ten years ago my grandmother started teaching me about making jam, in her kitchen in Scotland. I was really interested in it and we made jam that we sold at farmers' markets and on stalls at fairs. I had this idea that I wanted to make jam that was 100% fruit. I went to an open day that Waitrose were hosting, for potential new suppliers to be able to show their wares – it's like *The X-Factor* for groceries! Hundreds of people queue up outside and you each get ten minutes with the person at Waitrose who is responsible for your product line. I saw the senior jam buyer at Waitrose and they must have looked at this 16-year-old boy wearing his Dad's suit and thought, who is this kid?! My first pitch to Waitrose was just the idea, which they

liked but they told me to go away and work on the recipe, get a factory on board and develop a brand.

I spent a year convincing a factory to work with me. They were interested in my idea to re-invent the product and make jam – a very traditional product – without sugar and just with fruit. They heard that Waitrose were interested in my idea and that helped persuade them to get on board. I went back to Waitrose once I'd developed my product and the brand a bit more. I pitched to them my idea for Superman Jam, a superhero branded jam. It was another 'no' from Waitrose and I'll admit that was my lowest moment. They told me the factory I was using was too expensive and that I had too many exotic flavours; that I should stick to the simple, classic flavours like strawberry and raspberry. They also said the label didn't communicate well and the superhero brand wasn't working.

I had put all my love and money into the idea and it hadn't worked. My friends and family were supportive but equally quite protective of me and they told me after the second 'no' that it might be best to give up. People close to you will tell you your idea is great because no one wants to tell you your idea won't work; that's like telling someone their baby is ugly! The only way you really know if you have an idea that will work is when people part with their money to get it. Those are the people you need to canvass opinions from and whatever they tell you, that's the correct answer. I had belief in my idea and I knew I just had to listen to my customer. There were people out there telling me they wanted a jam made of 100% fruit and I knew that, in spite of the rejection, Waitrose were still interested in the idea.

So I persevered and started again. This time, I got a new factory to work with me; I created a new brand, a very simple brand design that focused on the fact that the jam was 100% fruit: SuperJam. Eighteen months after Waitrose had rejected my idea, they said yes. Because of my story – helped by my young age, I guess – I got a lot of media coverage. I was on *BBC Breakfast* and *GMTV*. The store-owner of my local supermarket told me he'd just sold 1,500 jars of SuperJam, which was unheard

of for that type of product, and I got a call from Tesco the same day, asking to stock SuperJam.

I thought the hard part would be getting a supermarket to take on the product and agree to stock it on their shelves but actually, the hardest part is getting people to take it off the shelf! I went to 100 Waitrose stores and stood there all day giving out samples and telling people about my jam. It worked – those people bought the jam and I realised that the closer you can be to the physical point of sale when you're marketing and talking about your product, the better. There is this idea of the 'abstract consumer' that you imagine when you're marketing your product, which is all well and good but I think you need to be selling something that you can honestly say you would happily buy yourself. You are also the consumer.

One thing I learned from an entrepreneur friend of mine when we were talking about packaging and brand concept is that all brands should have one message that they aim to get across, to keep it simple. When you're building a brand there's an element of emotional connection with your customer; people buy into something. I had a great story that went with the brand but I think there's a story behind every brand. Over time I've discovered the aspects of my story that people find most interesting and which bit journalists ask me about and those are the elements I focus on when I'm telling the story.

SuperJam is launching in the US in January and I'm also going on the QVC shopping channel to talk about SuperJam so that people can phone in and order it! I'm developing the idea for a SuperHoney business that brings in elements of education for kids on the ecology of beekeeping. We want to put beehives on roofs and encourage beekeeping as part of our SuperHoney product campaign.

If I received a huge cash injection tomorrow, I'd spend it on design. Of all the things I've put into SuperJam, that's the thing that paid off and I'd tell any startup to spend everything you can afford on design. I'm really thrilled that I've managed to create a brand that people love and also feel loyalty towards; they've been taking the product off the shelf for six years now. It's been an adventure for sure.

Lessons from SuperJam:

What Fraser's story tells us is that in pitching to Waitrose, the product stayed the same (and a lovely product too) but Fraser could talk about the product in several different ways. The first time Fraser told Waitrose the story of his jam, he was focused on just the values of the jam and was unsuccessful. The second time when Fraser tried to sell the jam through a superhero brand that would appeal to boys just like him, he was also unsuccessful. But when he told the story of the jam using the attributes and qualities that would relate to SuperJam's audience, he won. The recipe wasn't the answer and neither was a brand that didn't speak to his audience. Over time Fraser worked out how to present his authentic recipe in a way that communicated it to his intended audience. SuperJam as a simple brand communicates a lovely story clearly, therefore Fraser's asset is the brand he's built.

Brand is that residual thing left in the marketplace after you've stopped advertising, sometimes called brand value. If a company is for sale and you subtract all the things you can measure – all the assets that can be costed – there is still something left behind in the marketplace. The company still exists in the minds of customers and those customers have an understanding of what that business means or meant to them, whether good or bad.

The accounting profession doesn't know what to do with this element so they use the term 'goodwill value'. It's a way to describe that intangible stuff that remains after all the measurable assets have been taken away. The goodwill value is the brand value. The ultimate goal of any business is to have goodwill value and I use the word 'goodwill' to mean 'brand'.

The most important asset a business builds over time is a good brand. It is more important to the survival of the business than a stockpile of cash, lots of investors or great contracts with suppliers. A good brand can keep your

sales up when the economy around your business is faltering and it can give you new opportunities and expanded revenue opportunities daily when times are good. To build a good brand you must come good on the promise you make to customers every, single, day.

GET YOUR HANDS DIRTY

Try this: Decide which of your business assets you need to build.

1. Look at your list of assets. People who are going to invest in your business or lend you money in years to come will perceive this list of what you own, and the revenue the company can generate without you, as the value of your company.
2. Determine which assets have the most economic value in terms of the revenue they generate for your business. Perhaps you'll decide your designs and your customer database are most important when it comes to generating revenue.
3. Determine which assets you need to focus on building in order to generate more revenue. Do you need to add more people to your reseller list? Do you need to produce more designs? Do you need more annual contracts to deliver your service?
4. Make a plan for building the assets that make your business easier to grow.

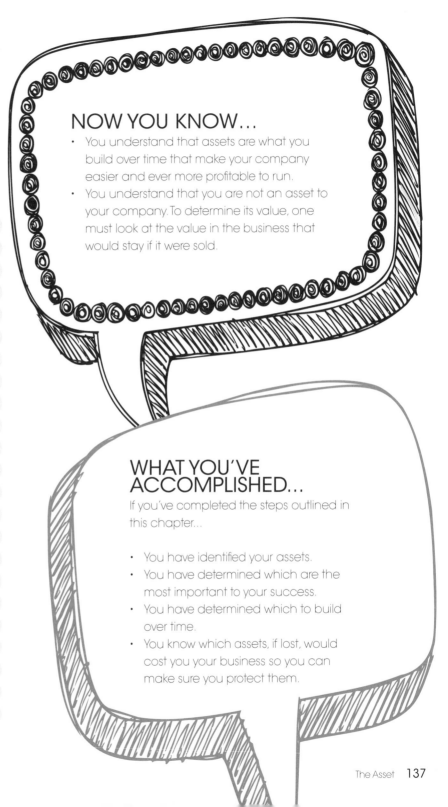

NOW YOU KNOW...

- You understand that assets are what you build over time that make your company easier and ever more profitable to run.
- You understand that you are not an asset to your company. To determine its value, one must look at the value in the business that would stay if it were sold.

WHAT YOU'VE ACCOMPLISHED...

If you've completed the steps outlined in this chapter...

- You have identified your assets.
- You have determined which are the most important to your success.
- You have determined which to build over time.
- You know which assets, if lost, would cost you your business so you can make sure you protect them.

CHAPTER 10: THE KEY COMPETENCY

WHAT MUST WE BE GOOD AT?

WHAT MUST WE BE GOOD AT?

JARGON BUSTER

Competencies are the skills that your business must be good at in order to prosper. Key competencies in a startup often depend on the expertise brought to the business by the founders.

A business has to have one *core* competency, plus a number of different people with a spread of competencies to cover all aspects of running the business.

Important business competencies

Heads up! I'm going to refer to the work of other visionaries here. There's a fantastic book called *The Discipline of Market Leaders: Choose Your Customers, Narrow Your Focus, Dominate Your Market* written by Michael Treacy and Fred Wiersema. I'm borrowing heavily from this book over the course of this chapter because the information it presents is relevant to startups even though the book was essentially written for established businesses. The *Discipline of Market Leaders* says that no company can succeed today by trying to deliver all things to all people. There are three different types of value disciplines: Operational Excellence, Product Leadership and Customer Intimacy.

OPERATIONAL EXCELLENCE

This competency is about creating efficiencies that deliver a given product or service more cost effectively than others. Amazon's Fulfilment service is an operational competency. They are leaders in delivering products worldwide and their customer satisfaction ratings are astronomical. Amazon can sell billions of products because Fulfilment by Amazon ensures people get what they paid for, quickly and without fuss.

If, as a startup, your core competency is operational excellence, it means that the supply chain is very important to your company. Your ability to run a lean, mean machine will be your focus.

PRODUCT LEADERSHIP

Nike and Apple do well at Product Leadership competency. For these companies it is all about excellence in product design and production. People often think Apple has great customer intimacy but actually its core competency is product leadership in that it has consistently, reliably, produced innovative products. Apple reinvented the music industry with the iPod, the mobile phone industry with the iPhone, the tablet computing industry with the iPad. Companies that depend on a product leadership competency are often driven not by what customers say they want, but what the visionaries within the enterprise (like the late Steve Jobs) know they want. Everything else follows behind. People will forgive Apple their failures for the sheer wonder of the product.

Is your startup going to be driven by the product? In that case, you'll need to spend your money and time on the invention and delivery of new products. Your product or service needs to embody innovations that make it much better than the competition.

CUSTOMER INTIMACY

If customer intimacy is your startup's core competency, your success will come from understanding the customer. You'll need highly trained staff and the ability to reach out to people. Startups often need a core competency in customer intimacy because they have to get their first sales under their belts before they can prove that they've got the best overall product or service. They need to find a particular customer, or kind of customer, that they can serve better than anyone else. Those early purchases from the business will fuel its growth.

Waitrose excels at customer intimacy, does a great job of making customers happy and as a company it communicates its values through its teams of educated and well-trained staff.

Waitrose knows that you can't be all things to all people, so they're clear about who they are and what they can do for their customer and their community. As a company you need to focus your energy and have a clear idea of where you are spending the most time and money. Which kind of company do you want to be to fulfil your proposition?

Important personnel competencies

To run a successful startup you don't need to be an expert in everything (what a relief!) but you do need to know the skills you have and the skills you need.

When you look at successful companies, the people who run the businesses (if they're doing it right) are a collection of colleagues with these different skills:

- People who can sell
- People who can deliver
- People who can analyse

People who sell, persuade vendors, creditors, partners, to work with the business.

People who delight in delivery enjoy getting things done, finishing the job and keeping customers on side.

People who analyse look at a thing, understand how it all works, put it together initially and maintain it over time.

A good business is a near perfect balance of all three competencies. All the three skills are required in every business. Frequently, one will be in the ascendant.

Which competency do you have? Once you can answer that question you can find people who can do the other stuff, the stuff you're not so good at...

Consider the promise you make to customers and what you need to deliver to them in order to make good on that promise.

1. List the competencies you need in order to make good on that promise.
2. List the largest risks your company faces. What core competencies are needed to reduce or eliminate those risks altogether?
3. List the people within your business who have those competencies. If you need competencies you don't currently have, think about how and where you can find people or services you can use that will fill in the gaps.

You need all three critical talents in your business early on although you do not, and probably should not, simply give a percentage of your business away to people with those skills. It is surprising how often an entrepreneur, grateful for any help at all in starting their business, will do this. Sometimes a co-founder is an appropriate addition to a business but be careful not to grant ownership of shares to people who join your business outright. Instead, work with a lawyer to draft an agreement that allows potential partners to gain ownership over time. This is called 'vesting' and it ensures that someone who promises to do something for a business actually has to deliver over several years to gain ownership. The agreement you draft should lay out specific tasks to be undertaken by each founder and exactly how fulfilment of obligations will be rewarded.

Generally speaking I'm not a fan of hiring people early in a company's life. While it does take a tiny village to get most enterprises off the ground, not all of the people you work with have to work for you full-time. You can hire a bookkeeper by the hour. You can find someone who knows how to sell who will agree to a percentage of each sale rather than drawing a regular salary. You don't have to compensate someone who helps your young business with ownership. Instead you can find someone who is willing to work for your enterprise on a part-time basis and on specific tasks. You can find someone who is starting their own business who you can work with as a first customer. You can find someone who can mentor you, or consult with you, in the missing skill set, so you can perform them yourself or with less skilled labour.

I'm a person who can sell; I'm the salesman. I'm outgoing and I'm outward facing. I don't take as much joy in delivering, so it's important to me to be surrounded by people who are good at organisational management and delivery. I attach myself to strong deliverers and I'll admit to you now that I need more analysts in my current business. I'd probably be more profitable if I hired an analyst, a reflective-type person, tomorrow.

The challenge of any business is when you overlap and have two people with the same skill set. Two great sales people will inevitably do their jobs differently and although they may both be able to generate sales, inevitably there will be conflict. Two accountants will be too conservative. Two delivery people, which includes wonderful craftspeople, will often generate great products but could fail at sales and cost tracking.

Good entrepreneurs often have some measure of all three of the core skills and usually excel at one. If, as an entrepreneur, you know that you don't have a particular skill and it's one you feel you desperately need, remember that no skill is impossible to acquire. There are books and courses that can teach you anything if you want to learn.

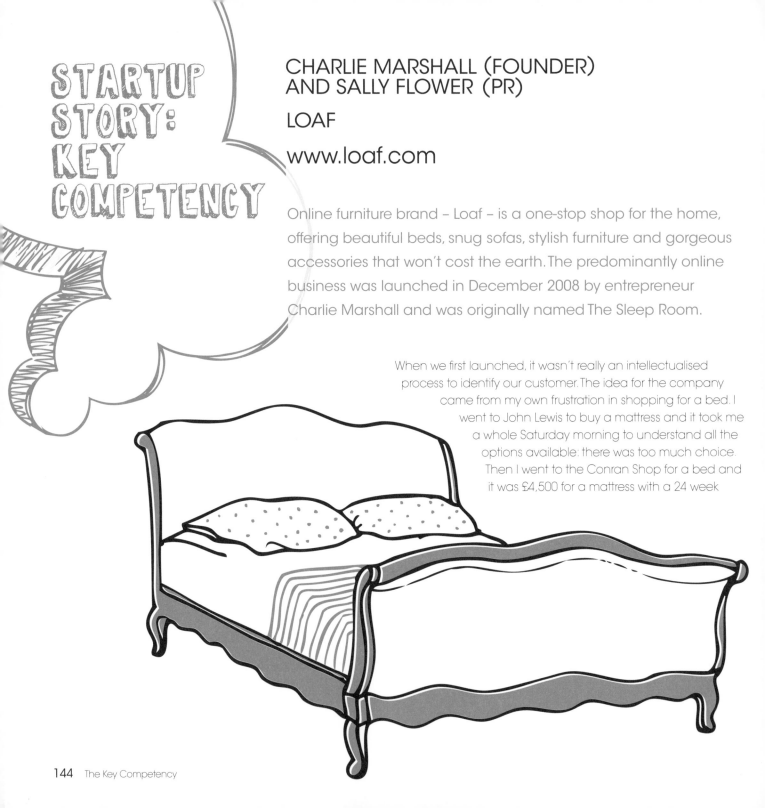

STARTUP STORY: KEY COMPETENCY

CHARLIE MARSHALL (FOUNDER) AND SALLY FLOWER (PR)

LOAF

www.loaf.com

Online furniture brand – Loaf – is a one-stop shop for the home, offering beautiful beds, snug sofas, stylish furniture and gorgeous accessories that won't cost the earth. The predominantly online business was launched in December 2008 by entrepreneur Charlie Marshall and was originally named The Sleep Room.

When we first launched, it wasn't really an intellectualised process to identify our customer. The idea for the company came from my own frustration in shopping for a bed. I went to John Lewis to buy a mattress and it took me a whole Saturday morning to understand all the options available: there was too much choice. Then I went to the Conran Shop for a bed and it was £4,500 for a mattress with a 24 week lead time. I felt that it shouldn't be that difficult or expensive to buy a bed and that there were probably other people out there, like me, equally frustrated. I decided to try and make the whole process as simple and transparent as possible.

I thought that our customers would be like me and to an extent they are, so the simplest way to communicate with them was to make the company's tone of voice, my voice. We started with 12 bed frames and one mattress, selling at a fraction of the high street cost but when I looked at sales of the 12 models, the more quirky beds that I would have in my house were selling in the bottom 15% and the more conventional stuff had become the bread and butter of our business. The criteria I ask now when I look at a product is less about trying to sell to people who have the same interior design taste as me and much more about whether it fits in with the Loaf look, as a special product with exceptional quality. It's been a steep learning curve to realise that the overriding criterion can't be whether I would I put it in my own home – although I do actually have many Loaf items in my house!

We have an approach that is different to our competitors'. We have to be experts in what we do and I know *everything* about our products. I've been to over 200 factories. Our team at Loaf are a certain type of person and we have a clear training programme to make sure that everyone in the team knows as much as I do about our

products. What John Lewis has that Loaf doesn't is their heritage. It enables people to trust them implicitly. We have to have the personal voice, we have to be slightly kooky, we have to be friends with our customers to try and gain their trust in a different way. We know we have to tick off certain fears that customers have because we're selling at a distance. We try to pre-empt the obvious worries customers have about whether we are trustworthy and reliable and whether the product will be good enough. One of the most important things we try to do is to make people feel that we're empathising with them.

We're not mass market, we're probably supplying the top 10% of the market. We have an agency that specialises in analytics and looks in detail at our sales figures as we get huge amounts of data about our customers each month. We know that 97% of people who order a fabric swatch from us are women, and that the figure drops to about 65% women when you analyse who does the purchasing. Our customers are aged 35–55, predominantly women that live in London and the South East, the more affluent areas of the country. Our customers are well-read, well-travelled, often university-educated and have an eye for good design. They can also smell bullsh*t a mile away so I decided right from the get-go that the best form

of marketing is honesty. We set out to be 'disarmingly honest' because a lot of marketing I see is quite deceptive.

I think there's been a huge breakdown in boundaries in the home, a move to open-plan living and a change in the way we live our lives – the rise of the home office, for example, and the decline of the traditional dining room. There's also a change happening in tandem, which is a change to the tone and conversation of business brands. When I started in business, newsletters were quite formulaic and just contained deals and offers as that was the norm. Nowadays I find language in business is less formal and more like the language we use with friends. That's the language we use in our newsletter because we're a very easy, casual brand.

One of the things that is a real mantra for me, I actually learned from my best friend who is an Oxford don. It is to really think about the question rather than leaping in too soon to try and find the answer. He taught me to think about the question and really condense it to the absolute crux of what is being asked: reduce it, reduce it, reduce it. I apply this thinking to the business all the time. We try to take time to work out what exactly it is that we are trying to do and then do it really well by doing it as simply as possible. We need to make it palatable for everyone.

We were slow to do email marketing, we only started that 12 weeks ago. We never send emails about '20% off' or 'here's our summer range' because we think about our customers as our friends and we ask ourselves, what would our friends want to receive from us? We look at our customers not as money machines but as people who we would want to talk to and we're careful not to inundate them. We make sure we treat our customers how we want to be treated ourselves.

The reality is that to do our job well is very difficult. It is not easy getting a piece of furniture – crafted from a live material (wood), often made in a part of the developing world – packaged, shipped to the UK, stored in our warehouse and then delivered and assembled within the right delivery hours to our customer. If one element of that process goes wrong the whole thing is ruined. We email all of our customers after we have delivered to them and we read our customers reviews avidly, we respond to them and if things aren't perfect we want to know why. We even created a playful widget called the 'crap-o-meter' to track and manage the team's stress levels when dealing with any tricky situations. It means I can see when one of my team is unfairly

burdened by calls and I can deal with it. I can also see if there are any common issues so we can fix them and improve our customer experience.

The consumer has got much more clout these days because of the rise in social media. But at the same time, I think the consumer is realising that a lot of reviewers are almost professional ranters. John Lewis has online reviews that get 3.5 out of 5 – and they're a great company! What we've found is that if we have a customer who complains a lot, if we give them what they want, they actually end up spending more money with us.

The hardest thing in our whole business is warehouse and distribution. It's a separate business in itself. We realised it would cost £300,000 less to open the business if we didn't do our own distribution to start with, so we looked around for a good distributor partner to manage it on our behalf. I bought a sofa from Sofa Workshop and had a good snoop around their distributor's warehouse. I saw the whole operation, met the owner and shook his hand. We liked the way that they operated, so we decided to build that relationship with them. Now if we have any problem with our distribution, we just call the owner as we have to trust that they will continue our positive relationship with our customers. As part of our communication with our customer, once they have placed their order with us we send them a 'thank you for your order' email with next steps and information about our delivery company, explaining that they are a nice, family-run company and we give out their contact details in case they want to get in touch. It means there isn't a dip in communication with our customer and we keep them informed at every stage.

The one part of our story we don't explicitly talk to our customers about is that about 40% of our stuff is made in China. People have a negative perception of China as a manufacturer but the truth of it is that in the West we no longer have the craft skills to carve furniture. I took my old French bed and sent it off to a factory in China to see if they could make the bed to the same standard. They produced a bed that was identical to the one I had sent them; the craftsmanship was incredible! We have product stories on our website and the one thing we do talk about to our customers is the carving schools and the craftsmanship near Shanghai – but we don't yet mention the word 'China'. I think there will come a time when consumers will be used to 'Made in China' in the same way as 'Made in Britain', without the negative association. We get our stuff made in family-run businesses in China, not huge enterprises but our challenge now is how to tell that story.

The good thing about beds is that they are expensive items so you don't need to sell too many of them to turn a profit but the bad thing from a sales perspective is that people only buy a bed once every five or ten years. We have over 98% of customers saying that

they had a really great service from us and are really pleased with their purchase but we realised, frustratingly, that we couldn't do any more for them until they return in a decade's time to buy a new bed! We've expanded our offering to other products and recently made the decision to offer our customers smaller products that they can potentially buy every couple of months. From next March we'll have over 156 new products, from bed-linen to floor rugs, kitchen tables and even kids' furniture.

NOW YOU KNOW...

- You understand that businesses as a whole, and individuals within a business, need specific skills to ensure a startup will thrive.
- You know what those competencies are and how to acquire them without giving your startup away in the process.

WHAT YOU'VE ACCOMPLISHED...

If you've completed the steps outlined in this chapter...

- You have identified the core competency your business needs in order to thrive.
- You have determined what critical competency you bring to your business.
- You have identified what competencies you need to acquire either by finding people to work with or by taking courses and reading books that can give you these skills.

Understand your value by drawing your business

It is often helpful to create and maintain a map of your business as you begin to analyse and build it.

- At the top, state your promise to customers.
- In the middle of the page, write your company name and define the industry it is in.
- On the far left write down everyone you buy from.
- On the far right write down everyone you sell to.
- Between you and your customers, put in your pricing model and the advertising, promotion, support, distribution and sales channels you will use to reach your customers.
- Add some detail to document the advantage your business has over its competitors, the characteristics of your market, etc. Tie each advantage to some aspect of your business model. Does it lower supplier costs? Does it allow you to increase your sales margins? Does it reduce competition? Does it help you reach your market quickly and cheaply?

Drawing your business helps you see its fundamentals and you'll find your diagram is handy when you need to present your enterprise to others.

EXAMPLE OF A BUSINESS MAP:

Suppliers

Hawaiian
Tropic
Johnson & Johnson
Australian Gold
Maui Babe

ADVANTAGE
We sell only premium brands.

Supplier Channels

Alibaba
Sunclub
Tan
International

ADVANTAGE
We buy direct from the manufacturer so our price is reasonable.

"WE SELL SUNTAN LOTION TO FAMILIES VISITING HAWAIIAN BEACHES"

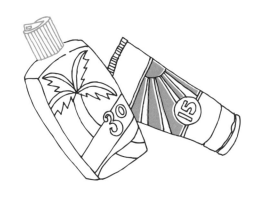

Our Company

Our pavement and beach vendors sell suntan lotion to people at the beach. We stock best selling products as well as 'natural' products, products for sensitive skin, and products for the youngest beach goers.

Sales Channels

Street vendors (school and college kids working during the summer)
Food carts and small vendors set up on the beach daily.
Hotels that face onto the beach sell our 'Welcome Basket' of sunning products to new arrivals.

Customers

Vacationing Couples
Newlyweds
Families with Children
Our customers generally stay in local hotels, don't shop in supermarkets that may undercut us, and value our carefully selected range of products.

ADVANTAGE
We don't have stores so our price stays low.

ADVANTAGE
We bring products directly to customers.

ADVANTAGE
Our customers enjoy both convenience and value.

THE PERKS OF BEING AN ENTREPRENEUR

- When you know how to start strong, successful, profitable businesses, what you do for a living always follows your interests. You can do what you love.
- You know how to evaluate other businesses and related investment opportunities to see if they are really sound. You will build wealth rather than debt as years go by.
- You can teach your children how to build successful businesses, and they can teach their children. Entrepreneurship runs in families because it is a skill that's easy to teach and easy to learn once you've mastered it.
- If you choose to work with or for others, you can choose businesses that you know will be successful because you will understand the fundamentals they must be built on.
- Best of all, you'll know that success has far less to do with 'hard work' than people think. It has more to do with a desire to understand and help people, a willingness to experiment and test assumptions and the courage to solve problems as and when they arise.
- I founded School for Creative Startups because I love starting and running good businesses and I don't think it's difficult, confusing or hard. I think, with the right training, a sense of humour and some determination, it's something most people can do.

NEXT STEPS: OVER TO YOU...

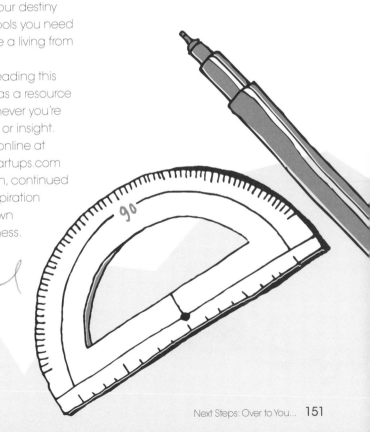

The purpose of this book is to help you test your business idea and to help your startup survive and prosper in its earliest days. As I said in the introduction, creative people frequently don't build businesses around their creativity because they believe that business is something that non-creative people do. My hope is that with this book, I have been able to remove that uncertainty and prove that starting a business is something that any of us can do.

Many of the world's best and most innovative businesses have been started by creative people; people who endeavoured to find a way to continue their art or craft and to be self-sustaining in the process. The contribution of the creative industries to the world cannot be measured solely in profits or employment (although they do generate millions and employ many). Our lives are enriched, our world is made better, when creative people design and deliver the products, services and solutions we all need.

Where you go from here is entirely your choice. You can put the book away, lay your creative business idea to rest and continue on with your life. Or you can take the idea that you have, which led to you reading this book in the first place, and begin the journey towards starting your own business and changing your life. What you can't do from this point on is ever say that you didn't start your business because you didn't know how to start it. You know now. You have everything you need should you wish to pursue your dream and the world should be full of people brave enough to do so.

My contribution is to put you in control of your life and your destiny and to give you all the tools you need to empower you to make a living from what you love doing.

I hope you enjoyed reading this book, and that it serves as a resource you come back to whenever you're looking for help, support or insight.

I invite you to join us online at www.schoolforcreativestartups.com for additional information, continued support and endless inspiration to help you build your own wonderful creative business.

Doug Richard

TERMS YOU NEED TO KNOW

You'll master many new terms as you build your business, but there are a few that you should know before you begin. Note that my definitions, written for entrepreneurs, may differ from those you have previously heard.

BRAND

Brand is a group of emotions and ideas that people associate with a product or service. For example, vodka is a product that people buy almost solely based on brand. It is a simple distilled beverage and people buy it almost exclusively on the basis of the price, the bottle, the packaging and the marketing they've seen for it. If you create a good brand you can charge more for what you sell.

CHANNEL

A channel is a means by which a business reaches its market. There are sales channels like retail stores and websites as well as support channels, product awareness channels, social media channels, and delivery channels. Creating, maintaining and growing good channels helps you sell to, deliver to and support your customers. Many of your company's channels will be businesses run by others.

COMPETITOR

A competitor is every business of any value that you could possibly identify as someone who is vying for the same business as you or eats into your market in some way. The world did not get to this point in human history without finding a way to meet the need or desire your product or service fulfils. While some entrepreneurs do manage to come up with a new innovation or invention that no one has thought of before, there are always other products or services that have previously met the same need. In fact, if you don't have competition you don't have a business worth investing time and effort in because you are trying to meet a need no one on Earth appears to have.

ENTREPRENEUR

An entrepreneur is a person who starts one or more businesses. Entrepreneurs are founders of the businesses they start. Sometimes entrepreneurs work alone, sometimes they work as members of a team. Many entrepreneurs start one business, make it successful, and then move on to start other businesses. These people are called serial entrepreneurs.

INDUSTRY

You and every business that competes with you make up an industry. Sometimes members of an industry work together on marketing campaigns that help sell a given type of product or service to the world or share the expense of asking legislators to create laws favourable to the kind of work you do.

MARKET

All the people who want to buy what you sell represent your market. They share a common need or desire that makes them value what you sell. They may also share other properties too. When you understand your market, their needs and desires, you know what they must hear in order to make a purchase decision. You know where to find them on- and offline and you are prepared to close the sale of a product or service you've designed to suit them.

REVENUE MODEL

Customers can pay for the products and services you sell in many ways. You can charge them a fixed price for something, sell them a subscription to it, or let them rent it for a specific period of time. Sometimes two types of customers will be needed to make a product or service feasible. A magazine sells ads to one group of their customers (advertisers) and subscriptions to a second group (readers). Sometimes a business delivers a service for free, then charges for the use of additional components of the service.

SUPPLIERS

Suppliers deliver the products and services that you need in order to to sell your products and services to your customers. Suppliers are always important to a business, and in some cases suppliers are the key to a company's value. Cartier is a diamond cartel so large that jewellery retailers will need a relationship with them to stay in business. A car repair business needs a good supplier for parts. A designer clothes company needs good suppliers for fabric and possibly fabrication of finished goods.

MORE ADVICE AND RESOURCES

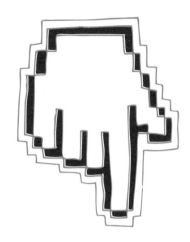

This list is not comprehensive – there are many more resources than I could ever begin to list, and requirements will vary from business to business. The tools listed here are some of my favourites and they meet the needs of many people who will use this book to design a strong, profitable, enterprise.

www.godaddy.com

A great place to register domain names and host websites. Search the Internet for Godaddy Wordpress for tools that let you build, launch and run an e-commerce enabled website. Godaddy provides great technical support for its customers. For more information on using Wordpress to create a website just search Amazon for books or YouTube for videos.

www.wordpress.org

A state of the art website building tool. You can build a commercial website in a few hours, or hire someone to do it for you just as quickly. GoDaddy has options that let you buy a Domain and set up a WordPress site in a few minutes. We are particular fans of the Subscriber 2 plug-ins. It sends people an email whenever you post something new on the site, effectively creating a 'newsletter' from every web post. There are several plug-ins that will allow you to incorporate PayPal buttons for content. Installation usually takes a couple of clicks. Applications can be removed just as easily.

www.linkedin.com

A great social media site for business professionals. You can find almost every executive or enterprise you might want to connect with through this site. Create a profile for yourself that describes your business, join up to 50 LinkedIn Groups that contain the people you want to contact, use the InMail tools to contact these professionals for free. You can run Ads on LinkedIn that very precisely target groups of people by location, industry, job title or job function. If you elect to run ads, use them to point to your LinkedIn profile, then purchase the cheapest LinkedIn account to see the profiles of those who visit that profile. That allows you to follow up with visitors to ask how you can be of service to them. This is a great way to reach out to any target market of business professionals.

www.facebook.com

The world's largest social media site featuring hundreds of millions of 'consumers' worldwide. To test market products and services on Facebook, create a profile for yourself and a page for your business. Offer those who visit your page and friend you (or message you) something of value for free. This may be a free ebook, a discount on something they want to buy from you, etc. Run ads through Facebook that drive people to your page and respond to those who contact you. Interview them, ask them questions about your competitors, ask for feedback on your product, etc. This is a very cost-effective way to reach many people in a given location, with a specific interest in a given product or service, very fast.

www.meetup.com

In many cities around the world, Meetup.com makes it easy to reach tens of thousands of people. Simply start a meet-up that offers free meetings to groups you want to target. Make the meetings educational seminars or networking events that deliver real value to your attendees. Never use a meet-up to sell to attendees. The backlash could be quite substantial. Do use Meetup events to network with customers and build long-term business relationships.

www.google.com/adwords

The fastest way to drive people to a website based on keywords, location and other demographics is through Google Adwords. Set up a domain and create a website that presents your product or service as if it were available for sale. When potential customers click the BUY button, display a form that lets people ask for more information and offers them a free voucher to buy what you are selling at a deep discount, when it becomes available. Modify the ad and the copy on the website to maximize the number of visitors you get and the number of people requesting more information or vouchers.

www.surveymonkey.com

This is a very handy tool for running surveys with your potential customers, contacts or event attendees. Use this tool to collect feedback from customers who have tried a given product or service. Incentivise them to complete the survey – what can you offer? Remember that anonymous feedback will allow people to be more honest in their responses.

IGNORE WHAT DOESN'T MATTER!

After you finish answering the Ten Questions you should have a solid understanding of how your business will work. Obviously you'll encounter twists and turns along the way, sometimes serious ones, but the foreseeable problems and opportunities will be understood and the risk of being blindsided, minimized.

You are now free to ignore what doesn't matter.

It is very easy when running a business, to get distracted by all the things you want to have or should have. Focus on what you *have* to have. Know what you sell, to whom, and why they value it. Gain visibility through creating effective marketing partnerships, keep your production costs as low as possible, get your pricing right. Be narrowly focused on the fastest growing target market you can reach. Ignore everything else.

If you do this effectively, you'll find you have time and resources to branch out to all the markets you'd like to serve and to design and deliver all the products and services those markets want.

INDEX

A DAVID & CHARLES BOOK
© F&W Media International, Ltd 2013

David & Charles is an imprint of F&W Media
International, Ltd
Brunel House, Forde Close, Newton Abbot, TQ12 4PU, UK

F&W Media International, Ltd is a subsidiary of F+W
Media, Inc
10151 Carver Road, Suite #200, Blue Ash, OH 45242, USA

Text and Designs © Doug Richard 2013
Layout © F&W Media International, Ltd 2013
Illustrations © Erin Rommel 2013
Case studies written by Laurie Jarmain

First published in the UK in 2013

Doug Richard has asserted his right to be identified as
author of this work in accordance with the Copyright,
Designs and Patents Act, 1988.

A catalogue record for this book is available from the
British Library.

ISBN-13: 978-1-4463-0273-6 paperback
ISBN-10: 1-4463-0273-3 paperback

Printed in Great Britain by TJ International Ltd, Padstow,
Cornwall for:
F&W Media International, Ltd
Brunel House, Forde Close, Newton Abbot, TQ12 4PU, UK

10 9 8 7 6 5 4 3 2 1

Publisher: Alison Myer
Desk Editor: Hannah Kelly
Project editor: Stuart Robertson
Proofreader: Lin Clements
Designer: Jennifer Stanley
Illustrator: Erin Rommel
Production Manager: Beverley Richardson

F+W Media publishes high quality books on a wide
range of subjects.
For more great book ideas visit:
www.stitchcraftcreate.co.uk